The WAY of the DISCIPLE

A Discovery Learning Approach to The Sermon on the Mount

Dr. Paul G. Leavenworth

Convergence Publishing
West Des Moines, Iowa
Copyright © 2014

Convergence Publishing
West Des Moines, IA 50265

Printed in the United States of America

Cover and Chapter Head Design by William Love
Book Design by WORDART, West Des Moines, IA

Table of Contents

Introduction

Bibliography
About the Author

Introduction

The Importance of the Right Foundation

The Way of the Disciple is designed to help followers of Christ (Disciples) to establish a Biblical foundation for life and leadership by doing an inductive Bible study of the Sermon on the Mount (Matthew 5-7). This Workbook is intended to facilitate "transformational learning" for establishing a foundation in "spirit and truth" (John 4:24) that will stand the test of time and help you meet the challenges of learning how to be "lovers in a dangerous time" (Bruce Cockburn, *Stealing Fire*, 1984). Jesus told his followers a story about the importance of foundations in Matthew 7. He said,

> **"Therefore everyone who hears these words of mine and puts them into practice is like a wise man who builds his house on the rock. The rain came down, the streams rose, and the winds blew and beat against that house; yet it did not fall, because it had its *foundation* on the rock. But everyone who hears these words of mine and does not put them into practice is like a foolish man who built his house on sand. The rain came down, the streams rose, and the winds blew and beat against that house, and it fell with a great crash."** Matthew 7:24-27, NIV (*italics* added)

Notice that the only difference between the wise and foolish builders was the ***foundation*** on which they built. The wise builder built on a foundation of "hearing and practicing," while the foolish builder heard, but did not put the words of Jesus into practice. They both built houses (the foolish builder's house may have been "nicer" than that of the wise builder, we do not know for sure), but when the storms of life came, only the wise builder's home remained standing.

What then (or who) is this foundation that Jesus is talking about? Paul identifies Christ as the "spiritual rock" (I Corinthians 10:4) in reference to the Old Testament story of the Exodus. The Psalms repeatedly state that the "Lord is my rock…" This is a statement that often refers to salvation (Psalms 89:26). In the New Testament, Jesus is called "a rock of offense" for those who refuse to believe that he is the promised Messiah (Romans 9:33 and I Peter 2:8).

Later on in Jesus' ministry, he further explains to his followers the importance of foundations when he says, "I have told you these things, so that **in me** you may have peace. In this world you will have trouble. But take heart! I have overcome the world" (John 16:33, NIV, **bold** added). So if Jesus is the rock on which wise people build their lives, why are so few in the modern Western church context doing it?

An Endangered Species

Have you noticed that there seems to be a major shift in the way people see the world? Over the last couple of decades, there has been a move away from a "Judeo Christian" worldview informed by Biblical values and principles to a more "progressive" or "post-modern" worldview based on personal experience and preferences. Several researchers and writers have documented this trend.

Thom Rainer in *The Bridger Generation* describes this worldview transition in America in terms of generational percentages that consider themselves "Bible-based believers" (p. 169):

Builders (born 1927-1945)	**65% Bible-based believers**
Boomers (born 1946-1964)	**35% Bible-based believers**
Busters (born 1965-1983)	**16% Bible-based believers**
Bridgers (born 1984 or later)	**4% Bible-based believers**

J. Robert Clinton in *Having a Ministry that Lasts* calls "Bible-centered" believers and leaders an "endangered species" (p. iii). Fewer folks (even those who claim to be followers of Jesus) know their Bible let alone try to live by its principles.

George Gallup and Timothy Jones in *The Next American Spirituality: Finding God in the 21st Century* describe this trend further when they state that:

> "At the beginning of the 20th century, the majority of Americans practiced their faith in at least a general framework that could be called Judeo Christian. They went from cradle to grave in a specific religious tradition. Now people are less likely to turn to church or religious institutions, more apt to depend on self-help books or tips from talk shows to arrive at their beliefs" (p. 38).

Gallup and Jones suggest that this trend has been fueled by cultural trends such as:

- **Unsettled violence**
- **Corruption in leadership**
- **Lifestyle gaps**
- **Alcohol and drug abuse**
- **Poverty**
- **Racism**
- **Family breakdown**
- **Consumerism and materialism**

They conclude that, "amid such tumult, Americans speak of their spirituality growing while they perceive… religion's impact diminishing… As a result, churches experience continuing decline and a seeming slide toward the cultural margins. With churches growing seemingly more irrelevant, people grow more confused and more anxious in their seeking" (p. 35).

Although there is a shift in worldview occurring in the American context, it is not all negative for those who embrace the more traditional Judeo Christian view. Gallup and Jones point out that with the decline in interest in "traditional" or "organizational" forms of religion has come an increased popularity in experiential spirituality (p. 42-43). They state that, "the interest in spirituality in itself is not an unalloyed cause for rejoicing. *But it provides a starting place for conversation*; it can bring life and fresh energy to stale custom; it can open people to the transforming presence of an enduringly real God" (p. 46, *italics* added).

Along these lines, George Barna in *Think Like Jesus* states that, "few Americans currently possess a biblical worldview, most are immersed in daily exercises of covert worldview training via the mass media, public law, public school education, the Internet, and conversations with peers" (p. 58). Barna further points out that worldview is important because, "*you become what you believe*" (p. 56, *italics* added).

This is why becoming a Bible-centered leader is so important and strategic for "such a time as this" (Esther 4: 14). To quote Barna again, he says that, "developing a strong Bible-based foundation from which to think and act is the only reliable safeguard against the complete demise of our culture, the loss of meaning and purpose in life, and the rejection of all that God holds dear and significant" (p. 57-58).

A Great Opportunity

"The Bible says" is a "politically incorrect" statement in a post-modern context, but I will use it because it is basic to my worldview. So, the Bible says that when people have, "no revelation, [they] cast off restraint, but blessed is he who keeps the law" (Proverbs 29:19, NIV). In other words, when people turn away from God and his revelatory standards, moral chaos will follow.

This fact was carefully recorded in graphic details in the Old Testament story of Israel and has been repeated again and again throughout history. Remember, worldview matters because, "*you become what you believe*" (Barna). If you believe a lie (even a really cleaver counterfeit) you will eventually experience the fallout of a faulty foundation (Matthew 7), but the promise of the Bible is that "the truth will set us free" (John 8:32) from deception and the enslaving consequences that follow. This is why becoming a Bible-centered leader is so important for our personal lives, relationships, and ministries.

The author of Hebrews puts it this way, "Jesus has become the guarantee of a *better* covenant" (Hebrews 7:22, NIV, *italics* added). The word better is used about a dozen times in Hebrews to emphasize this point. Being Bible-centered disciples and leaders is a better way to live life! The word used here (*kreisson*) means "<u>stronger</u>, more powerful."

The Apostle Paul puts it still another way when he calls true followers of Jesus, "Christ's *ambassadors*, as though God were making his appeal through us" (II Corinthians 5:10, NIV, *italics* added). Jesus' taught his disciples to pray, "[God's] kingdom come, [his] will be done *on earth* as it is in heaven…" (Matthew 6: 10, NIV, *italics* added).

Are you getting this? We, his *ambassadors*, have the opportunity to *demonstrate* (and share, if given an appropriate opportunity) his truth to a world that has lost its way and desperately needs to see (and know) that there is a *better* way to live life! Bible-centered leaders, through love, humility, and service will have great opportunities to engage people in "loving conversations" about foundational issues of worldview in the days ahead as the American culture "reaps the whirlwind" of "casting off restraint."

IDEA Approach to Transformational Learning

The Way of the Disciple is formatted using the **IDEA** approach to transformational learning. The goal of the **IDEA** approach is to facilitate the "gracious work" of God through his word and spirit to transform us "into his likeness with ever increasing glory…" (II Corinthians 3:18, NIV).

The first chapter of this workbook is an introduction to the Gospel of the Kingdom and discipleship. Each chapter after that will have four sections:

- **Introduction (I)** – various translations and paraphrases of the passage to be studied

- **Discovery (D)** – study questions to help you better understand the passage

- **Explanation (E)** – exegetical notes for the passage to help you interpret the passage

- **Application (A)** – questions to help you discern how to apply this passage to your life and leadership

The Bible study approach used in *The Way of the Disciple* is the inductive study method. According to Walter Henrichsen and Gail Jackson (*Studying, Interpreting, and Applying the Bible*) inductive Bible study involves:

1. **Observation** – "What do I see?"

2. **Interpretation** – "What does it mean?"

3. **Correlation** – "How does this relate to what the rest of the Bible says?"

4. **Application** – "What does it mean to me?"

There are many study helps available but I start my students out with a study Bible (also see biblegateway.com for several translations or paraphrases) and *The Three-In-One Bible Reference Companion* (1982, Thomas Nelson Publishers, ISBN 0-7852-0972-7) which is a combined Concordance, Topical Index, and Dictionary that is referenced to the King James Version of the Bible. This is a simple and inexpensive way to begin to study the Bible. Also, you may want to check out www.mystudybible.com for a free and easy-to-use computer Bible study resource. You can certainly add to your Bible study library later as you become more proficient in your Bible study skill set.

Some Pointers

This workbook is not meant for everyone. It is not an easy way to gain insights about the Sermon on the Mount (Matthew 5-7). Actually, it is an invitation to do some time consuming "digging" into the meaning and application of each passage through the use and development of Bible study skills that will be useful for studying additional passages in the Bible. Here are a few pointers that may help make this workbook more useful for you.

1. In the **Introduction (I)** section I give you the King James (KJV) translation as the header under the title for the chapter along with two other translations: the New International (NIV), the New American Standard (NASB); and one paraphrase: the Message (Message). I have included translations that are more accurate to the original Greek manuscripts as well as a paraphrase that is less accurate but easier to read so that you get multiple perspectives for each passage as you study. Read these over prayerfully a couple of time before starting the **Discovery (D)** section. You may also want to access the biblegateway.com site to read other translations and paraphrases.

2. In the **Discovery (D)** section I give you several inductive Bible study questions. Most of these questions will have to do with observation but I also ask interpretation, correlation, and application questions. I would encourage you to use *The Three-In-One Bible Reference Companion* (Concordance, Topical Index, and Dictionary) resource book here especially when I ask you to look up other passages in the Bible that reference the main word or phrase that you are studying. This is

called correlation and is important so that you get an understanding of what the rest of the Bible says about the word or phrase. Also, you may want to check out www.mystudybible.com for a free and easy-to-use computer Bible study resource. I have also included principles of interpretation and application in Appendix E: Inductive Bible Study Methodology to help you develop guidelines for accurate interpretations and appropriate applications.

3. In the **Explanation (E)** section I give you my exegetical (word-by-word) notes from my study of the Sermon on the Mount (Matthew 5-7). I include the Greek word, part of speech, verb tense, literal translation, and descriptions from commentators. I do not have any formal training in the original languages of the Bible (Hebrew, Aramaic, and *koine* Greek) and do not claim to be a Greek scholar. I am pretty much self-taught so that I can use the language tools developed by scholars for general use by folks like me. Here is a list of the primary language tools that I used for my exegetical notes that I include in this section.

GREEK RESOURCES:
- Davis, William H., *Beginner's Grammar of the Greek New Testament*, 1923, Harper & Row Publishers
- Han, Nathan, *A Parsing Guide to the Greek New Testament*, 1971, Herald Press
- *The Analytical Greek Lexicon*, 1975, Zondervan Publishing House
- *The Zondervan Parallel New Testament in Greek and English*, 1975, Zondervan Publishing House

WORD STUDIES:
- Kittles, Gehard and Gerhard Friedrich (editors), translated from German to English by Geoffrey Bromiley, *Theological Dictionary of the New Testament*, 1985, Eerdmans Publishing
- Vine, W. E., *Expository Dictionary of the New Testament*, 1966, Thomas Nelson Publishers

COMMENTARIES:
- Barclay, William, *The Gospel of Matthew*, Volume 1, 2001, John Knox
- Boice, James Montgomery, *The Sermon on the Mount*, 1972, Zondervan
- Bonhoeffer, Dietrich, *The Cost of Discipleship*, 1973, Macmillan
- Briscoe, Stuart, *Tough Truths for Today's Living*, 1978, Word Publishing
- Carson, D.A., *The Sermon on the Mount*, 1978, Baker Books
- Jones, E. Stanley, *The Christ of the Mount*, 1981, Abingdon
- Lloyd-Jones, Martyn, *Studies in the Sermon on the Mount*, 1989, IVP
- Stott, John, *The Message of the Sermon on the Mount*, 1978, IVP

Greek is a very precise language. The verb tenses are particularly revealing. A summary of Greek verbs is available at http://www.ntgreek.org/learn_nt_greek/verbs1.htm. If you are not interested in this degree of detail you can still benefit from the definitions of the Greek words and the brief descriptions by various commentators that I include in this section.

4. In the **Application (A)** section I include a couple of questions that encourage you to clarify, summarize, and develop plans for application of what you are learning. Without application you may get smarter but you will not necessarily experience transformation into the character and likeness of Christ. Bible study is not just about gaining information. It is primarily about transformation. Remember Paul's words about Scripture in II Timothy 3:16-17:

    "All Scripture is God-breathed and is useful for teaching, rebuking, correcting and training in righteousness, so that the man [woman] of God may be thoroughly equipped for every good work." (NIV)

    The Bible is more than words on a page. It is God's special revelation that shows us "the way, the truth, and the life" (John 14:6) that, along with the Holy Spirit, empowers us to be "true worshippers" (John 4:24) who can experience "abundant life" (John 10:10) here and now and "eternal life" (John 3:16) in the life to come.

5. Lastly, I would encourage you to work through this workbook with a partner or in a small accountability group. Doing it together may help you keep from getting overwhelmed and possibly quitting. Together you can support and encourage one another while gaining helpful insights from other's observations, interpretations, correlations, and applications.

Take your time and prayerfully and carefully read, study, discuss, apply, and evaluate your progress. Remember that becoming a Bible-centered leader is not an objective as much as it is a process or lifestyle. Over the years you will be transformed and God will reveal the "meat" of his word if you remain "teachable" (Hebrews 5:11-14). Blessings!

CHAPTER 1

The Gospel of the Kingdom and Discipleship

> **"And this gospel of the kingdom will be preached in the whole world as a testimony to all nations, and then the end will come."** Matthew 24:14, NIV

Introduction (I):

These words of Jesus to his disciples describe the defining events that must happen before he comes again. In this passage, Jesus tells his closest followers about the events that will lead up to his "coming and the end of the age" (Matthew 24:3). These events include:

- **Deception** (verses 4-5 and 11)
- **Wars and rumors of wars** (verses 6-7)
- **Famines** (verse 7)
- **Earthquakes** (verse 7)
- **Persecution** (verses 9-10)
- **Increase of wickedness** (verse 12)
- **Lack of love** (verse 12)

But Jesus tells his disciples that these events are only "the beginning of birth pangs" (verse 8). These events set the stage for the completion of Jesus' commission to his disciples that he gave them a few days later (after his death on the cross and his resurrection from the dead):

> **"All authority in heaven and on earth has been given to me. Therefore go and make disciples of all the nations, baptizing them in the name of the Father and of the Son and of the Holy Spirit, and teaching them to obey everything I have commanded you. And surely I am with you always, to the very end of the age."** Matthew 28:18-20, NIV

Do you see the connection between "the gospel of the kingdom" and "mak[ing] disciples of all the nations?" The gospel of the kingdom provides the overriding context for understanding discipleship. We must first understand what the gospel of the kingdom is before we can fully understand what discipleship is all about.

The Gospel of Matthew describes Jesus' early ministry in the following way:

> **"Jesus went throughout Galilee, teaching in their synagogues, preaching the good news [gospel] of the kingdom, and healing every disease and sickness among the people."** Matthew 4:23, NIV

The word kingdom (*basileia*) is used over 100 times in the New Testament: Matthew (50 times), Mark (19 times), Luke (44 times), John (4 times), Acts (8 times), Paul's epistles (13 times), Hebrews (3 times), James (1 time), II Peter (1 time), and Revelation (6 times). This word is used predominantly in the Synoptic Gospels (Matthew, Mark, Luke), but is also used throughout the New Testament. It is a major concept in the Gospels and the rest of the New Testament.

Although we will focus on the New Testament passages on the kingdom of God (also kingdom of "heaven," "Christ," etc.), it is also a prominent concept in the Old Testament as well (used over 100 times). George Eldon Ladd, in his book *The Gospel of the Kingdom*, states that the, "primary meaning of both the Hebrew word *malkuth* and the Greek word *basileia* in the New Testament is rank, authority and sovereignty by a king… The kingdom of God is His kingship, His rule, His authority" (p. 19 and 21).

So Jesus' message of good news (gospel) was about the kingdom. What, exactly, is the gospel of the kingdom? To answer this, let's take a look at Jesus' gospel proclamations:

- **"Repent, for the kingdom of heaven is near."** Matthew 4:17, NIV

- **"'The time has come,' he said. 'The kingdom of God is near. Repent and believe the good news!'"** Mark 1:15, NIV

- **"I must preach the good news of the kingdom of God to the other towns also, because that is why I was sent."** Luke 4:43, NIV

- **"I tell you the truth, no one can enter the kingdom of God unless he is born of water and the Spirit."** John 3:5, NIV

All these passages make reference to Jesus' proclamation of the gospel of the kingdom.

Matthew makes reference to the kingdom of heaven because he is writing to Jewish people, while the others refer to the kingdom of God because they are writing to Gentile peoples. A closer look at these passages reveals that:

1. **The gospel of the kingdom is good news;**
2. **It requires belief;**
3. **It requires repentance; and**
4. **Meeting these requirements results in being born again.**

Let's take a look at each of these a little closer. First, ***the gospel of the kingdom is good news.*** Since mankind's fall in Genesis 3, there has been a promise from God that he would send a deliverer (Genesis 3:15) who will set us free from our sin. The primary word used in the Bible for this is salvation. Salvation (*yeshuah* in Hebrew and *soteria* in Greek) refers to, "the act or state of deliverance from danger, especially deliverance by God from the penalty and power of sin" (Bromiley, editor, *The International Standard Bible Encyclopedia*, p. 287).

Salvation requires an act that meets God's standards for both love and justice. This was met though the life, death, and resurrection of Jesus Christ, the promised deliverer (also referred to as the *Messiah*). In Hebrews, the author says that, "Although he was a son, he learned obedience from what he suffered and, once made perfect, he became the source of eternal salvation for all who believe him…" (Hebrews 5:8-9, NIV).

Sinful mankind needs a deliverer and God has provided one through his son Jesus Christ:

> **"Who, being in very nature God, did not consider equality with God something to be grasped, but made himself nothing, taking the very nature of a servant, being made in human likeness. And being found in appearance as a man, he humbled himself and became obedient to death – even death on a cross! Therefore God highly exalted him to the highest place and gave him the name that is above every name, that at the name of Jesus every knee shall bow, in heaven and on and under the earth, and every tongue confess that Jesus Christ is Lord, to the glory of God the Father."**
> Philippians 2:6-11, NIV

Jesus paid the full price that sin required. God warned mankind that if they chose to try to live their lives apart from him (and his kingdom), it would result in death (Genesis 2:16-17). But because of God's love (see John 3:16), he gave his son Jesus Christ as the payment for our sin. That is why the gospel of the kingdom is such good news!

Second, *it requires belief.* This gift of salvation from God must be received through belief. Belief is not just intellectual agreement to a set of facts about Christ, but involves recognizing our need for salvation and receiving God's provision by faith. Belief is much more than agreeing to some sort of doctrinal statement, although solid doctrine is important. Belief involves a heartfelt acknowledgment of our slavery to sin and our need for his atoning work on our behalf.

Atonement is central to the Bible's teaching on man's need and God's provision. Atonement refers to, "the work Christ did in his life and death to earn our salvation" (Wayne Grudem, *Bible Doctrine*, p. 480). Grudem further describes atonement as involving four needs of mankind and four provisions from God. Mankind's needs include (p. 255):

1. **We deserve to die as the *penalty* for sin.**
2. **We deserve to bear God's *wrath* against sin.**
3. **We are *separated* from God by sin.**
4. **We are in *bondage* to sin and the kingdom of Satan.**

These four needs are addressed through Jesus' atoning death on the cross, and meet God's requirements for justice and love. Through Christ we can realize:

1. **Freedom from the *penalty* of sin because of his perfect sacrifice (SACRIFICE).**
2. **Freedom from the *wrath* of God through his payment for our sin (PROPITIATION).**
3. **Restoration from *separation* to proper relationship with God (RECONCILIATION).**
4. **Deliverance from the slavery of *bondage* to sin and the freedom not to sin (REDEMPTION).**

Belief in the finished work of Jesus Christ on the cross should fill our hearts with gratitude and joy, resulting in repentance.

Our third characteristic of Jesus' gospel of the kingdom is that *it requires repentance*. Repentance (*nacham* in the Hebrew and *metanoeo* in the Greek) refers to, "a heartfelt sorrow for sin, a renouncing of it, and a sincere commitment to forsake it and walk in obedience to Christ" (Grudem, *Bible Doctrine*, p. 492). Repentance literally means, "to change one's mind, resulting in a radical change of direction in one's lifestyle."

Notice that Jesus' gospel of the kingdom requires both belief and repentance. Grudem is helpful here. He says that, "it is important to realize that mere sorrow for one's actions, or even deep remorse over one's actions, does not constitute genuine repentance unless it is accompanied by a sincere decision to forsake sin that is being committed against God… Repentance is something that occurs in the heart and involves the whole person in a decision to turn from sin" (p. 310).

This is critical for our understanding of discipleship and what it means to be a true follower of Christ. James puts it this way, "What good is it, my brothers, if a man claims to have faith but has no deeds? Can such faith save him?" (James 2:14, NIV).

James goes on to state that, "faith by itself, if it is not accompanied by action, is dead" (James 2:17, NIV). The kind of belief and repentance that Jesus is requiring are two sides of the same coin. They are part of the same dynamic that can lead to being born again.

Our fourth characteristic is that the gospel of the kingdom **leads to being born again**. Jesus told the Pharisee Nicodemus that, "no one can see the kingdom of God unless he is born again" (John 3:3). Nicodemus' response was predictable, "How can a man be born when he is old?" (verse 4).

Jesus' response is found in the well known passage of John 3:16-18:

> **"For God so loved the world that he gave his one and only Son, that whoever believes in him shall not perish, but have eternal life. For God did not send his Son into the world to condemn the world, but to save the world through him. Whoever believes in him is not condemned, but whoever does not believe stands condemned already because he has not believed in the name of God's one and only Son"** (NIV).

True belief in the person of Jesus Christ results in a radical transformation likened to being born anew. Paul describes this process, "Therefore, if anyone is in Christ, he is a new creation; the old has gone, the new has come!" (II Corinthians 5:17, NIV).

What good news! We do not have to remain trapped in our selfishness or defined by our circumstances. We have a new life in which we are, "more than conquerors through him who loved us" (Romans 8:37, NIV). See *Appendix A: The Presence of the Future* for further information about how the kingdom of God is active in the life of the disciple and the church.

Discovery (D):

1. Review this **Introduction (I)** section and respond to the following questions:

    What does "kingdom" mean in the Bible?

    What was Jesus' gospel message?

    What were the four characteristics of Jesus' gospel of the kingdom message?

2. Briefly define in your own words the following Biblical concepts:

    Salvation –

    Atonement –

Sacrifice –

Propitiation –

Reconciliation –

Redemption –

Repentance –

3. Describe in your own words what it means to be "born again."

4. Discussion questions (for further thought):

    What has been your understanding of the gospel?

    What have you learned about the gospel of the kingdom that Jesus proclaimed?

    Why do you think that some believers fall away while others stay the course in their Christian faith?

Explanation (E):

In this section, let us take a look at what the Bible has to say about discipleship. Disciple (*mathetes*) is predominately a New Testament concept (used over 100 times in the Gospels and Acts) with roots in the Old Testament. The basic meaning of disciple is, "taught or trained one" (Young, *Analytical Concordance to the Bible*, p. 257). Although the word disciple is not used in the Old Testament, the concept of training through apprenticeship to a specific Rabbi is well established. According to *The International Standard Bible Encyclopedia* (Bromiley, editor):

> "Although the vocabulary of teaching and learning is prominent in the OT, the disciple figure is virtually absent… In the rabbinic realm, the talmid [student] devoted himself to learning Scripture and the religious tradition, above all that tradition which is passed on through his teacher… In this system, both teacher and student typically sat in an appointed room, and the teacher taught by question, and through repetition and memorization" (p. 947).

Although there are similarities between the rabbinic training model of the Old Testament and the discipleship model of Jesus, there are also some major differences:

1. In the rabbinic model, students could pick the Rabbi they wanted to study under. In Jesus' discipleship model, he selected the disciples he wanted to train.

2. In the rabbinic model, most learning was academic and took place in a classroom. In Jesus' discipleship model, most learning took place within the context of real life situations as they traveled and ministered together.

3. In the rabbinic model, the content to be learned was the traditional understanding of Scripture that the Rabbi advocated. In Jesus' discipleship model, the content was intended to transform the lives of the disciples.

Sanctification

Let's examine this idea of sanctification (holy living) a little closer. What is meant by sanctification? Sanctification (*qadesh* in the Hebrew and *hagiazo* in the Greek) means, "to be separate, set apart" (Young, *Analytical Concordance to the Bible*, p. 834). Vine (*Vine's Complete Expository Dictionary of Old and New Testament Words*) describes "sanctification" (Greek noun form, *hagiasmos*) as:

> "(a) separation to God, I Corinthians 1:30; II Thessalonians 2:13; I Peter 1:2;

(b) the course of life befitting those so separated, I Thessalonians 4:3, 4, 7; Romans 6:19, 22; I Timothy 2:15; Hebrews 12:14. Sanctification is that relationship with God into which men [women] enter by faith in Christ, Acts 26:18; I Corinthians 6:11, and to which their sole title is the death of Christ, Ephesians 5:25, 26; Colossians 1:22; Hebrews 10:10, 29; 13:12." (p. 545)

Sanctification for a disciple involves at least three qualities:

1. **Sanctification involves a "separation" to God from sin, the fallen world system, and the influences of the devil.**

2. **Sanctification involves the work of the Holy Spirit in transforming the believer from the inside out.**

3. **Sanctification involves obedience to the Word and the leading of the Spirit in the individual life choices of the believer.**

With this in mind, let me define discipleship:

Discipleship is a life transforming relationship with Christ as savior and lord involving change in character, perception and behavior that reflects the life and ministry of Christ who came to love and save the lost.

Discipleship involves five components:

1. **Lordship salvation**
2. **Life changing relationship with Jesus Christ as Lord**
3. **Change in heart that will lead to a change in perception and behavior**
4. **Life of love for others** (especially the needy)
5. **Participating in sharing the "good news" with people**

Discipleship is a process that will involve many ups and downs as we learn to follow Christ in the fullness of what the Bible says about following him. We will need grace to grow and endure as disciples, but, remember that we have everything we need because of who Christ is and what he did for us. Paul says it this way, "I can do everything through [Christ] who gives me strength" (Philippians 4:13, NIV).

In conclusion, Francis Cosgrove, in his book *Essentials of Discipleship*, has developed "A Biblical Profile of a Disciple" (p. 15-16) involving eleven qualities and functions. These include:

1. A disciple is **a learner** – open and teachable.
   * Proverbs 9:8-10, Matthew 4:19, John 6:60-66

2. A disciple **puts Christ first** [Lordship] in all areas of his/her life.
   * Matthew 6:9-13, Luke 9:23, John 13:13, II Corinthians 5:15

3. A disciple is committed to **a life of purity** and is taking steps to separate him/herself from sin.
   * I Corinthians 6:19-20, Ephesians 4:22 – 5:5, Colossians 3:5-10, I Thessalonians 4:3-7, Titus 2:12-14

4. A disciple has a daily [**regular**] **devotional time** and is developing his/her prayer life.
   * Psalms 27:4; 42:1-2, Mark 1:35, Luke 11:1-4, I Thessalonians 5:17-18, James 1:5-7; 5:16

5. A disciple demonstrates faithfulness and a desire to **learn and apply the Word of God** through hearing it preached and taught, reading it frequently, studying it, memorizing it, and meditating on it.
   * John 8:31, Acts 2:42; 17:11, Colossians 3:16, II Timothy 2:15

6. A disciple has **a heart for witnessing,** gives his/her testimony with clearly, and presents the gospel regularly with increased skill.
   * Matthew 28:18-20, Acts 1:8; 5:42; 14:21-23; 22:14-15; Romans 1:16; I Corinthians 15:3-4, I Thessalonians 2:4

7. A disciple **attends church regularly** to worship God, to have spiritual needs met, and to make a contribution to the body [community] of believers.
   * Psalms 122:1, Acts 16:5, I Corinthians 12:12-27, Colossians 1:15-18, Hebrews 10:25

8. A disciple **fellowships regularly** with other believers, displaying love and unity.
   * John 17:22-26, Acts 2:44-47; 4:31-33, Ephesians 4:1-3, Hebrews 10:24, I John 1:1-3

9. A disciple demonstrates **a servant's heart** by helping others in practical ways.
   * Mark 10:42-45, Acts 6:1-4, II Corinthians 12:15, Philippians 2:25-30, I Thessalonians 2:8-9

10. A disciple **gives regularly** and honors God with his/her finances.
    * Haggai 1:6-9, Malachi 3:10-11, I Corinthians 16:1-2, II Corinthians 8-9, Philemon 14

11. A disciple demonstrates the **fruit of the Spirit** by an attractive relationship with Christ and his/her fellow man.
    * Acts 16:1-2, I Corinthians 13:4-7, Galatians 5:22-23, I Peter 2:18-23, II Peter 1:5-8

Working out our salvation by becoming mature disciples is a work of grace involving endurance and perseverance (see James 1:2-4) through life's many challenges, disappointments, and opportunities. Although discipleship is our own responsibility, we also need others. Very few of us, if any, can make it alone. We need one another to "bear our burdens" (Galatians 6:2) if we are going to mature as disciples. Humility (I Peter 5:6) and "abiding" (John 15:5) in Christ are essential to this process, but the comfort, encouragement, prayers, and accountability of other disciples is also critical if we are to become the true disciples that God desires for us to be.

Application (A):

Application is the "heart" of the matter if we want to become a true follower of Jesus who can empower others and lead like Jesus. To this end, please prayerfully and carefully respond to the following questions:

Please rank yourself on the eleven characteristics of "A Biblical Profile of a Disciple" using the following rating scale:

1 – not at all   2- seldom   3 – occasionally   4 - regularly   5 – almost always

1. Learner – open and teachable: 1   2   3   4   5
   Comments:

2. Christ as first [Lordship]:   1   2   3   4   5
   Comments:

11

3. Committed to a life of purity: 1   2   3   4   5
    Comments:

4. Daily devotional life: 1   2   3   4   5
    Comments:

5. Faithfulness to learn and apply the   1   2   3   4   5
    Word of God:
    Comments:

6. Witnesses to others: 1   2   3   4   5
    Comments:

7. Attends church: 1   2   3   4   5
    Comments:

8. Fellowships with other believers: 1   2   3   4   5
    Comments:

9. Helps others in practical ways: 1   2   3   4   5
    Comments:

10. Gives tithes and offerings: 1   2   3   4   5
    Comments:

11. Demonstrates the fruit of the Spirit:　　　1　　　2　　　3　　　4　　　5
　　Comments:

What insights about the Gospel of the Kingdom and discipleship have you gained from this chapter?

While praying through this list of insights, ask God which of these you are already applying and which you need to start applying. Try to identify strengths and weaknesses, and prioritize which weaknesses God wants you to work on.

Identify the top priority issue that God wants you to work on and formulate a study/application plan to allow God to graciously begin his transforming work in your heart. What is God's top priority issue and how are you going to cooperate with him in this?

Is there a mentor or accountability partner who can help you by giving wise counsel, praying, encouraging, holding you accountable, etc.? Who is it and how/when will you contact him/her?

CHAPTER 2

Matthew 5:1-2 – Overview and Context

^{5:1} And seeing the multitudes, he went up into a mountain: and when he was set, his disciples came unto him. ² And he opened his mouth, and taught them, saying, (KJV)

Introduction (I): Go to biblegateway.com for additional translations and paraphrases.

(NIV) ^{5:1-2} Now when Jesus saw the crowds, he went up on a mountainside and sat down. His disciples came to him, and he began to teach them.

(NASB) ^{5:1} When Jesus saw the crowds, He went up on the mountain; and after He sat down, His disciples came to Him. ² He opened His mouth and began to teach them, saying,

(Message) ^{5:1-2} When Jesus saw his ministry drawing huge crowds, he climbed a hillside. Those who were apprenticed to him, the committed, climbed with him. Arriving at a quiet place, he sat down and taught his climbing companions. This is what he said:

Discovery (D): Study Guide for Matthew 5:1-2 – Context

Read the passage in the KJV and respond to the following questions:

1. What is Jesus doing?

2. What is the context of these verses?

- Matthew 4:17 –

- Matthew 4:18-22 –

- Matthew 4:23-25 –

3. Who is Jesus teaching to?

4. What is your interpretation and application of this passage?

Explanation (E):

Overview of Matthew: The Gospel of Matthew Portrays Jesus as the Messiah.

Author: Matthew, Son of Alphaeus, a tax gatherer who was one of the Twelve.

Date and Setting: Matthew was probably written (between 58-68 A.D.) after Mark and before the Roman conquest of Jerusalem in 70 A.D. Matthew apparently used Mark as a primary source for his gospel.

Theme and Purpose: Matthew wrote his gospel to the Jews to showing them that Jesus was the Messiah from his life and ministry as fulfillment of Old Testament sources (53 OT quotes). He begins his gospel with a genealogy tracing Jesus back to Abraham and frequently refers to him as the son of David. About 60% of Matthew's gospel contains the spoken (red letter) words of Jesus.

Key Word: Messiah ('the Anointed One")

Literary Structure: Matthew was writing to Jewish people so he uses the phrase "Kingdom of Heaven" instead of "Kingdom of God" when referring to Christ as King and to his Kingdom. After 400 years with no prophet, the Jews were desperate for God to fulfill his promises of the coming of Messiah and the establishing of his Kingdom. Matthew was placed first in the New Testament Canon because it is a natural bridge between the Old and New Testaments.

Survey: There are five sections in Matthew (each ending with the phrase "when Jesus had ended" – 7:28; 11:1; 13:53; 19:1; and 26:1):

1. The Sermon on the Mount (5:3 - 7:27);
2. Instructions to the Disciples (10:5-42);
3. Parables of the Kingdom (13:3-52);
4. Terms of Discipleship (18:3-35); and
5. The Olivet Discourse (24:4 – 25:46).

Outline:

Part One: The Presentation of Messiah (1:1 – 4:11)
Part Two: The Proclamation of Messiah (4:12 – 7:29)
Part Three: The Power of Messiah (8:1 – 11:1)
Part Four: The Progressive Rejection of Messiah (11:2 – 16:12)
Part Five: The Preparation of Messiah's Disciples (16:13 – 20:28)

Part Six: The Rejection of Messiah (20:29 – 27:66)
Part Seven: The Resurrection of Messiah (28:1-20)

Context of The Sermon on the Mount: Matthew 5:1-2

I. THE MEANING OF DISCIPLE (*mathetes*) – Vine (*Expository Dictionary of N.T. Words*) defines disciple as "a learner (from *manthano*, to learn, from a root *match-*, indicating thought accompanied by endeavor), in contrast to *didaskalos*, a teacher; hence it denotes one who follows one's teaching…" (p. 316)

Phillips (*The Making of a Disciple*) describes discipleship as, "a teacher-student relationship, based on the model of Christ and His disciples, in which the teacher reproduces the fullness of life he has in Christ in the student so well, that the student is able to train others to teach others." (p. l5)

Ortiz (*Disciple*) says that, "a disciple is one who follows Jesus Christ. But because we are Christians does not necessarily mean we are His disciples, even though we are members of His Kingdom. Following Christ means acknowledging Him as Lord; it means serving Him as slave." (p. 9)

Watson (*Called and Committed*) points out that Christian discipleship is more than a relationship of a student to a subject or an apprentice to a trade; it is a relationship of being, "fully committed to their master as well as to his message." (p. 6)

II. THE CALLING OF THE DISCIPLE - In Matthew 4:18-22 Jesus calls His disciples to "come, follow me" (see Mark 1:16-20, Luke 5:1-11, John 1:35-51).

COME (*deuro*) - In this passage *deuro* literally means, "come now."

FOLLOW (*opiso*) - In this passage *opiso* literally means, "at one's back" or to follow behind or after.

Barclay (*GOM*, Vol. l) says of the calling that, "what Jesus needs is ordinary folk who will give him themselves. He can do anything with people like that." (p. 78)

III. THE COST TO THE DISCIPLE - Jesus spells out the conditions of discipleship in Luke l4:25-35 (also see Matt. 10:37-38). In this passage Jesus uses the phrase "cannot be my disciple" three times to emphasize the conditions of true discipleship. These conditions are: 1) His Lordship in relationships; 2) His Lordship in plans and ambitions; and 3) His Lordship over possessions.

HATE (*miseo*) - The verb "hate" in Luke 14:26 is present active indicative that means the ongoing fact of hating. Vine states that *miseo* means, "malicious and unjustifiable" feelings toward others" but that *miseo* is also used to communicate a "relative preference for one thing over another, by way of expressing either aversion from or disregard for, the claims of one person or thing relative to those of another…" (p. 198)

CARRY (*bastazo*) - The verb "carry" in Luke 14:27 is present active indicative that means the ongoing fact of bearing under something. Vine states that *bastazo* means, "to bear a burden, whether physically, as of the cross, John l9:l7, or metaphorically in respect of sufferings endured in the cause of Christ, Luke 14:27…" (p. 100)

GIVE UP (*apotasso*) - The verb "give up" in Luke 14:33 is present active indicative that means the ongoing fact of saying farewell to or taking leave of something. Vine states that *apotasso* means, "to forsake, Luke 14:33…the stronger meaning is 'getting rid of a person.'" (p 78)

IV. THE MANIFESTATION OF THE DISCIPLE - Jesus gave his disciples a new commandment to "love one another" (John 13:34). He said that by this, "all men will know that you are my disciples" (13:35). Later on that same evening he gave his disciples this new commandment and prayed for them, "that all of them may be one" (John 17:21). Again Jesus said that because of this, "the world may believe that you have sent me" (17:21).

LOVE (*agape*) - In John 13:35, *agape* is the direct object of the verb *echo* (present subjunctive) that literally means, "to have love." Vine states that *agape* is used in the N.T., "(a) to describe the attitude of God toward His Son, John 17:26; the human race, generally, John 3:16, Rom. 5:8; and to such as believe on the Lord Jesus Christ, particularly, John 14:21; (b) to convey His will to His children concerning their attitude one toward another, John l3:34, and toward all men, I Thes.3:12, I Cor. 16:14; II Pet. 1:7; (c) to express the essential nature of God, I John 4:8." (p. 20-21)

BE ONE (*heis*) - In John l7:21, "one" is the object of the verb *eimi* (present subjunctive) that literally means, "that all may be one."

Schaeffer (*The Mark of the Christian*) says, "we cannot expect the world to believe that the Father sent the Son, that Jesus claims are true, and that Christianity is true, unless the world sees some reality of the oneness of true Christians." (p. 15)

V. THE MISSION OF THE DISCIPLE - Jesus' commission to his disciples at the end of his earthly ministry was to "go and make disciples of all nations" (Matt. 28:16-20). Based on his authority (28:18) and his promise to be with his disciples always (28:20), the process of making disciples involves baptizing and teaching others to obey all of the commandments of Christ (28:19-20).

MAKE DISCIPLES (*matheteuo*) - In Matthew 28:19, the verb *matheteuo* is a first person aorist active imperative that means making disciples at a point in time.

Coleman (*The Master Plan of Evangelism*) states that, "this mission is emphasized even more when the Greek text of the passage is studied, and it is seen that the words 'go,' 'baptize,' and 'teach' are all participles which derive their force from the one controlling verb 'make disciples.'" (p. 108)

Application (A):

What insights about discipleship have you gained from this chapter?

While praying through this list of insights, ask God which of these you are already applying and which you need to start applying. Try to identify strengths and weaknesses, and prioritize which weaknesses God wants you to work on.

Identify the top priority issue that God wants you to work on and formulate a study/application plan to allow God to graciously begin his transforming work in your heart. What is God's top priority issue and how are you going to cooperate with him in this?

Is there a mentor or accountability partner who can help you by giving wise counsel, praying, encouraging, holding you accountable, etc.? Who is it and how/when will you contact him/her?

CHAPTER 3

Matthew 5:3-12 – Beatitudes

5:3 Blessed are the poor in spirit: for theirs is the kingdom of heaven.

5:4 Blessed are they that mourn: for they shall be comforted.

5:5 Blessed are the meek: for they shall inherit the earth.

5:6 Blessed are they which do hunger and thirst after righteousness: for they shall be filled.

5:7 Blessed are the merciful: for they shall obtain mercy.

5:8 Blessed are the pure in heart: for they shall see God.

5:9 Blessed are the peacemakers: for they shall be called the children of God.

5:10 Blessed are they which are persecuted for righteousness' sake: for theirs is the kingdom of heaven.

5:11 Blessed are ye, when men shall revile you, and persecute you, and shall say all manner of evil against you falsely, for my sake.

5:12 Rejoice, and be exceeding glad: for great is your reward in heaven: for so persecuted they the prophets which were before you. (KJV)

Introduction (I): Go to biblegateway.com for additional translations and paraphrases.

(NIV) He said: 5:3 "Blessed are the poor in spirit, for theirs is the kingdom of heaven. 4 Blessed are those who mourn, for they will be comforted. 5 Blessed are the meek, for they will inherit the earth. 6 Blessed are those who hunger and thirst for righteousness, for they will be filled. 7 Blessed are the merciful, for they will be shown mercy. 8 Blessed are the pure in heart, for they will see God. 9 Blessed are the peacemakers, for they will be called children of God. 10 Blessed are those who are persecuted because of righteousness, for theirs is the kingdom of heaven.

11 "Blessed are you when people insult you, persecute you and falsely say all kinds of evil against you because of me. 12 Rejoice and be glad, because great is your reward in heaven, for in the same way they persecuted the prophets who were before you.

(NASB) 5:3 "Blessed are the poor in spirit, for theirs is the kingdom of heaven. 4 "Blessed are those who mourn, for they shall be comforted. 5 "Blessed are the gentle, for they shall inherit the earth. 6 "Blessed are those who hunger and thirst for righteousness, for they shall be satisfied. 7 "Blessed are the merciful, for they shall receive mercy. 8 "Blessed are the pure in heart, for they shall see God. 9 "Blessed are the peacemakers, for they shall be called sons of God. 10 "Blessed are those who have been persecuted for the sake of righteousness, for theirs is the kingdom of heaven.

11 "Blessed are you when people insult you and persecute you, and falsely say all kinds of evil against you because of Me. 12 Rejoice and be glad, for your reward in heaven is great; for in the same way they persecuted the prophets who were before you.

(Message) 5:3 "You're blessed when you're at the end of your rope. With less of you there is more of God and his rule. 4 "You're blessed when you feel you've lost what is most dear to you. Only then can you be embraced by the One most dear to you. 5 "You're blessed when you're content with just who you are—no more, no less. That's the moment you find yourselves proud owners of everything that can't be bought. 6 "You're blessed when you've worked up a good appetite for God. He's food and drink in the best meal you'll ever eat.

24

[7] "You're blessed when you care. At the moment of being 'care-full,' you find yourselves cared for.
[8] "You're blessed when you get your inside world—your mind and heart—put right. Then you can see God in the outside world.
[9] "You're blessed when you can show people how to cooperate instead of compete or fight. That's when you discover who you really are, and your place in God's family.
[10] "You're blessed when your commitment to God provokes persecution. The persecution drives you even deeper into God's kingdom.

[11-12] "Not only that—count yourselves blessed every time people put you down or throw you out or speak lies about you to discredit me. What it means is that the truth is too close for comfort and they are uncomfortable. You can be glad when that happens—give a cheer, even! — for though they don't like it, I do! And all heaven applauds. And know that you are in good company. My prophets and witnesses have always gotten into this kind of trouble.

Discovery (D): Study Guide for Matthew 5:3-12 – Beatitudes

Read the passage in the KJV and respond to the following questions:

1. (5:3-12) What does the word "Blessed" mean? (Look up at least three other passages that use this word or phrase)

2. (5:3) What does "poor in spirit" mean? (Look up at least three other passages that use this word or phrase)

3. (5:3) What does "kingdom of heaven" mean? (Look up at least three other passages that use this word or phrase)

4. (5:4) What does "mourn" mean? (Look up at least three other passages that use this word or phrase)

5. (5:4) What does "comforted" mean? (Look up at least three other passages that use this word or phrase)

6. (5:5) What does "meek" mean? (Look up at least three other passages that use this word or phrase)

7. (5:5) What does "inherit the earth" mean? (Look up at least three other passages that use this word or phrase)

8. (5:6) What does "hunger and thirst after righteousness" mean? (Look up at least three other passages that use this word or phrase)

9. (5:6) What does "filled" mean? (Look up at least three other passages that use this word or phrase)

10. (5:7) What does "merciful" mean? (Look up at least three other passages that use this word or phrase)

11. (5:7) What does "obtain mercy" mean? (Look up at least three other passages that use this word or phrase)

12. (5:8) What does "pure in heart" mean? (Look up at least three other passages that use this word or phrase)

13. (5:8) What does "see God" mean? (Look up at least three other passages that use this word or phrase)

14. (5:9) What does "peacemakers" mean? (Look up at least three other passages that use this word or phrase)

15. (5:9) What does "children of God" mean? (Look up at least three other passages that use this word or phrase)

16. (5:10) What does "persecuted for righteousness" mean? (Look up at least three other passages that use this word or phrase)

17. (5:10) Why do you think Jesus repeated "kingdom of heaven" (verses 3 and 10)?

18. (5:11-12) What do these verses teach about persecution and the proper response?

19. (5:3-12) What pattern(s) do you see about attitudes and behaviors in the Beatitudes?

20. (5:3-12) What is your interpretation and application of this passage?

Explanation (E):

Matthew 5:3 - Blessed are the poor in spirit, for theirs is the kingdom of heaven.

BLESSED (*makarios*) - In Matthew 5:3 and following (verses 3-12), the word *makarios* is nominative masculine plural meaning literally "blessed ones." Vine (*Expository Dictionary of N.T. Words*) states that *makarios* comes "from the root *mak-*, meaning large, lengthy, found in *makros*, long, *makios*, length, hence denotes to pronounce happy, blessed... In the beatitudes, the Lord indicates not only the characters that are blessed, but the nature of that which is the highest good." (p. 133)

Barclay (*GOM*, Vol. l) describes *makarios* as the Greek word "which specially describes the gods. In Christianity there is a god-like joy... *Makarios* then describes that joy which has its secret within itself, that joy which is serene and untouchable, and self-contained, that joy which is completely independent of all the chances and changes of life." (p. 89)

Jones (*The Christ of the Mount*) points out that, "the word 'blessed' is more than joyful; it means literally 'not subject to fate,' 'deathless.' It depicts the kind of life that rises above the fated mechanism of earthly life into moral and spiritual freedom." (p. 53)

Boice (*The Sermon on the Mount*) states that, "when Jesus spoke these words He was telling His disciples that they could be deeply, spiritually, and profoundly happy and how they could maintain this happiness even in the midst of life's disappointments and hard times." (p. 17)

POOR (*ptochos*) - In Matthew 5:3, the word *ptochos* is nominative masculine plural that literally means "poor ones." Robertson (*Word Picture in the N.T.*) points out that there are two Greek words commonly used to describe the poor. *Penes* means "to work for one's daily bread and so means one who works for a living." *Ptochos* "implies deeper poverty than *penes*." (p. 40)

Barclay (*GOM*, Vol. l) states that *ptochos*, "describes absolute and abject poverty. It is connected with the root *ptossein*, which means to crouch or to cower; and it describes the poverty which is beaten to its knees." (p. 90)

Stott (*SOM*) concludes that, "to be 'poor in spirit' is to acknowledge our spiritual poverty, indeed our spiritual bankruptcy, before 'God." (p. 39)

SPIRIT (*pneuma*) - Vine writes that *pneuma* "primarily denotes the wind (akin to *pneo*, to breathe, blow); also breath, then, especially the spirit, which, like the wind, is invisible, immaterial and powerful." (p. 62)

Lloyd-Jones (*Sermon on the Mount*) concludes that what is meant by being poor in spirit is a "complete absence of pride, a complete absence of self-assurance and self-reliance. It means a consciousness that we are nothing in the presence of God. It is nothing, then, that we can produce; it is nothing that we can do in ourselves. It is just this tremendous awareness of our utter nothingness as we come face to face with God." (p. 50)

Bonhoeffer (*The Cost of Discipleship*) describes poverty of spirit as "privation is the lot of the disciples in every sphere of their lives. They are the 'poor' *tout court* (Luke 6:20). They have no security, no possessions to call their own, not even a foot of earth to call their home, no earthly society to claim their absolute allegiance. Nay more, they have no spiritual power, experience or knowledge to afford them consolation or security. For his sake they have lost all. In following him they have lost even their own selves, and everything that could make them rich. Now they are poor - so inexperienced, so stupid, that they have no other hope but him who called them." (p. 120)

KINGDOM (*basileia*) - Vine points out that *basileia* means the sovereignty and dominion of God and/or the territory or people over whom God rules. (p. 294)

Driver (*Kingdom Citizens*) states that, "followers of Jesus are the ones who choose to be poor in a world which is oriented in the opposite direction. The truly humble person views reality from the best perspective, the perspective of the kingdom..." (p. 60)

Barclay (*GOM*, Vol. I) comments that, "the Kingdom of God is a society where God's will is as perfectly done on earth as it is in heaven. That means that only he who does God's will is a citizen of the Kingdom; and we can only do God's will when we realize our own utter helplessness, our own utter ignorance, our own inability to cope with life, and when we put our whole trust in God." (p. 92)

Matthew 5:4 - Blessed are those who mourn, for they will be comforted.

BLESSED (*makarios*) - see description for blessed in Matthew 5:3. *The Amplified Bible* describes *makarios* as "happy, spiritually prosperous (with joy life- and satisfaction in God's favor and salvation, regardless of their outward conditions)."

MOURN (*penthos*) – In Matthew 5:4, *penthos* is a nominative plural present participle meaning literally "mourning ones." Vine (*Expository Dictionary of N.T. Words*) states that *penthos* means 'to mourn for, lament, is used (a) of mourning in general, Matt. 5:4; 9:15; Luke 6:25; (b) of sorrow for the death of a loved one, Mark 16:10; (c) of mourning for the overthrow of Babylon and the Babylonian system, Rev. 18:11... (d) of grief for those in a local church who show no repentance for evil committed, II Cor. 12:21...' (p. 87)

Barclay (*GOM*, Vol. 1) points out that *penthos* "is the strongest word for mourning in the Greek language. It is the word that is used for mourning for the dead, for the passionate lament for one who was loved... It is defined as the kind of grief that takes such a hold on a man that it cannot be hid. It is not only the sorrow which brings an ache to the heart, it is the sorrow which brings the unrestrainable tears to the eyes." (p.93) Barclay further comments that, "Christianity begins with a sense of sin. Blessed is the man who is intensely sorry for his sin, the man who is heart-broken for what his sin has done to God and to Jesus Christ, the man who sees the cross and who is appalled by the havoc brought by sin." (p. 95)

Carson (*The Sermon on the Mount*) comments that, "at the individual level, this mourning is a personal grief over personal sin. This is the mourning experienced by a man who begins to recognize the blackness of his sin, the more he is exposed to the purity of God." (p. 18)

Miller (*The Christian Way*) concludes that, "the mourners of whom He speaks in this second beatitude are those gripped by the agony of repentance. And repentance, true repentance, is an agony." (p. 28)

COMFORTED (*parakleo*) - The verb comforted in Matthew 5:4 is third person plural future passive indicative that means the future fact of being comforted. Vine states that *parakleo* means "a calling to one's side (*para*, beside, *kaleo*, to call); hence, either an exhortation, or consolation, comfort..." (p. 207)

Jones (*The Christ of the Mount*) comments that, "comfort is made up of two words, *con*, 'with', and *fortis* 'strength' - literally, 'strengthened by being with'. In choosing the way of the cross we find ourselves in an intimacy of companionship with Christ, who toils up that same road, and there in that way we hear words that make the heart sing amidst it's sacrifice." (p. 67)

Lloyd -Jones (*Sermon on the Mount*) concludes that, "if we truly mourn, we shall rejoice, we shall be made happy, we shall be comforted. For it is when a man sees himself in this unutterable hopelessness that the Holy Spirit reveals unto him the Lord Jesus Christ as his perfect satisfaction. Through the spirit he sees that Christ has died for his sins and is standing as his advocate in the presence of God. He sees in Him the perfect provision that God has made and immediately he is comforted." (p. 60)

Matthew 5:5 - Blessed are the meek, for they will inherit the earth.

BLESSED (*makarios*) – See description for blessed in Matthew 5:3. *The Amplified Bible* describes *makarios* as "happy, spiritually, prosperous (with life-joy and satisfaction in God's favor and salvation, regardless of their outward conditions."

MEEK (*prautes*) – In Matthew 5:5, *prautes* is a nominative masculine plural which literally means "meek ones." Vine (*Expository Dictionary of N.T. Words*) describes *prautes* as having "deeper significance than in non-scriptural Greek writings, it consists not in a person's outward behavior only; nor yet in his relations to his fellow men… Rather it is an inwrought grace of he soul; and the exercises of it are first and chiefly towards God. It is the temper of the spirit in which we except His dealings with us as good, and therefore without disputing or resisting; it is closely linked with the word *tapeinophrosune* (humility), and follows directly on it, Eph. 4:2; Col 3:12… it is only the humble heart which is also meek, and which, as such, does not fight against God and more or less struggle and contend with Him. This meekness, however, being first of all a meekness before God, is also such in the face of men, even of evil men, out of a sense that these, with insults and injuries which they may inflict, are permitted and employed by Him for the chastening and purifying of His elect' (Trench, Syn., xlii)." (p. 55-56) Vine further comments that *prautes* is the "fruit of power" and "the opposite of self-assertiveness and self-interest…" (p. 56)

Bonhoeffer (*The Cost of Discipleship*) describes the meek as those who possess "no inherent rights of their own to protect its members in the world, nor do they claim such rights, for they are meek, they renounce every right of their own and live for the sake of Jesus Christ.

When reproached, they hold their peace, when treated with violence, they endure it patiently, when men drive them from their presence, they yield their ground. They will not go to law to defend their rights, nor make a scene when they suffer injustice, nor do they insist on their legal rights. They are determined to leave their rights to God alone..." (p. 123)

Lloyd-Jones (*Sermon on the Mount*) states that, "meekness is essentially a true view of oneself, expressing itself in attitude and conduct with respect to others. It is therefore two things. It is my attitude toward myself; and it is an expression of "poor in spirit" and "mourning". A man can never be meek unless he has seen himself as a vile sinner. Those other things must come first. But when I have the true view of myself in terms of poverty of spirit, and mourning because of my sinfulness, I am led to see that there must be an absence of pride." (p. 68-69)

INHERIT (*kleronomeo*) – The verb "inherit" in Matthew 5:5 is a third person plural future indicative that means the future fact of inheriting. Vine states that *kleronomeo* means "to receive by lot (*kleros*, a lot, *nomomai*, to possess); then, in a more general sense, to possess oneself of, to receive as one's own, to obtain." (p. 258)

Stott (*SOM*) suggests that, "the godless may boast and throw their weight about, yet real possession eludes their grasp. The meek on the other hand, although they may be deprived and disenfranchised by men, yet because they know what it is to live and reign with Christ, can enjoy and even 'possess' the earth, which belongs to Christ. Then on the day of 'regeneration' there will be 'new heavens and a new earth' for them to inherit." (p. 44)

EARTH (*ge*) – Vine describes *ge* as "the earth as a whole, the world, in contrast, whether to the heavens, e.g. Matt. 5:18, 35, or the Heaven, the abode of God, e.g. Matt. 6:19..." (p. 13)

Matthew 5:6 - Blessed are those who hunger and thirst for righteousness, for they will be filled.

BLESSED (*makarios*) – See the description of blessed in the Matthew 5:3. *The Amplified Bible* describes *makarios* as "happy, spiritually prosperous (with life-joy and satisfaction in God's favor and salvation, regardless of their outward conditions)."

HUNGER (*peinao*) – In Matthew 5:6, *peinao* is a nominative masculine plural present participle meaning the ongoing state of hungering. Kittle (*Theological Dictionary of the N.T.*) defines *peinao* as "to be hungry, or avidly to desire something." (p. 820)

Barclay (*GOM*, Vol. 1) comments that, "the hunger which this beatitude describes is no genteel hunger which could be satisfied with a mid-morning snack; the thirst of which it speaks is no thirst which could be slaked with a cup of coffee or an iced drink. It is the hunger of the man who is starving for food, and the thirst of the man who will die unless he drinks." (p. 99-100)

THIRST (*dipsao*) – In Matthew 5:6, *dipsao* is a nominative masculine plural present participle that means the ongoing state of being thirsty. Thus, in this beatitude *peinao* and *dipsao* literally mean "hungering ones" and "thirsting ones." Kittle defines *dipsao* as "to be thirsty or to long for something." (p. 177)

Barclay (*GOM*, Vol. 1) comments that, "this beatitude is in reality a question and a challenge. In effect it demands, 'How much do you want goodness? Do you want it as much as a starving man wants food, and as much as a man dying of thirst wants water?' How intense is our desire for goodness? Most people have an instinctive desire for goodness, but that desire is wistful and nebulous rather than sharp and intense; and when the moment of decision comes they are not prepared to make the effort and the sacrifice which real goodness demands." (p. 100)

RIGHTEOUSNESS (*dikaiosune*) – In Matthew 5:6, *dikaiosune* is an accusative singular (direct object) meaning "right standing" or "right action." Vine (*Expository Dictionary of N.T. Words*) defines *dikaiosune* as "the character or quality of being right or just; it was formerly spelled 'rightwiseness,' which clearly expresses the meaning. It is used to denote an attribute of God, e.g., Rom. 3:5, the context of which shows that 'the righteousness of God' means essentially the same as His faithfulness, or truthfulness, that which is consistent with His own nature and promises…" (p. 298)

Jones (*The Christ of the Mount*) comments that, "this desire for righteousness becomes a hunger that eats up the lesser hungers of one's life, until the man himself is eaten up with this all-inclusive hunger." (p. 72)

Bonhoeffer (*The Cost of Discipleship*) states that, "not only do the followers of Jesus renounce their rights, they renounce their righteousness too." (p. 123-124)

Boice (*The Sermon on the Mount*) concludes that, "first, he must desire righteousness. Second, he must desire a perfect (and, therefore, a divine) righteousness. Third, he must desire it intensely. That is he must desire it enough to abandon all hope of achieving salvation by this own efforts, and cling instead to the efforts made for him by God." (p. 43-44)

FILLED (*chortazo*) – In Matthew 5:6, *chortazo* is third person plural future passive indicative that means the fact of future fulfillment for those who are hungering and thirsting after righteousness. Vine defines *chortazo* as "to fill or satisfy with food." (p. 320)

Stott (*SOM*) suggests that, "in this life our hunger will never be fully satisfied, nor our thirst fully quenched… our hunger is satisfied only to break out again." (p. 46)

Carson (*The Sermon on the Mount*) states that, "the context [of Matthew 5:6] demands that we understand the blessing to mean 'will be filled with righteousness.' The Lord gives this famished person the desires of his heart. This does not mean that the person is now so satisfied with the righteousness given him that his hunger and thirst for righteousness are forever vanquished… So there is a sense in which we are satisfied with Jesus and all he is and provides. Nevertheless, there is a sense in which we continue to be unsatisfied." (p. 22-23)

Matthew 5:7 - Blessed are the merciful, for they will be shown mercy.

BLESSED (*makarios*) – See the description of blessed in Matthew 5:3. *The Amplified Bible* describes *makarios* as "happy, spiritually prosperous (with life-joy and satisfaction in God's favor and salvation regardless of their outward conditions)."

MERCIFUL (*eleos*) – In Matthew 5:7, *eleos* is a nominative masculine plural that means "merciful ones." Vine (*Expository Dictionary of N.T. Words*) defines *eleos* as "the outward manifestation of pity; it assumes need on the part of him who receives it, and resources adequate to meet the need on the part of him who shows it." (p. 60)

Barclay (*GOM*, Vol. 1) states that "the Greek word for merciful is *eleemon*. But, as we have repeatedly seen, the Greek of the New Testament as we possess it goes back to the original Hebrew and Aramaic. The Hebrew word for mercy is *chesedh*; and it is an untranslatable word. It does not mean only to sympathize with a person in the popular sense of the term; it does not mean simply to feel sorry for someone in trouble. *Chesedh*, mercy, means the ability to get right inside the other person's skin until we can see things with his eyes, think things with his mind, and feel things with his feelings… It denotes a sympathy that is not given, as it were from outside, but which comes from a deliberate identification with the other person, until we see things as he sees them, and feels things as he feels them… Sympathy is derived from the two Greek words, *syn*, which means together with, and *paschein*, which means to experience or to suffer. Sympathy means experiencing things together with the other person, literally going through what he is going through." (p. 103)

Briscoe (*Tough Truths for Today's Living*) comments that, "mercy is God withholding from us what we do deserve. Merciful kindness is seeing someone reap the results of his rash actions, and being heart broken over their pain. It's the opposite of the one who gloats over the misfortunes of others." (p. 38)

MERCY (*eleeo*) – In Matthew 5:7, *eleeo* is a third person plural future passive indicative that means the fact of future mercy for those who are merciful to others. See the definition of *eleos* above. Vine says that, "grace describes God's attitude toward the law breaker and the rebel; mercy is His attitude toward those who are in distress." (p. 61)

Galilea (*The Beatitudes*) comments that, "to be merciful, according to the teaching of Christ, means to commit ourselves to aiding the needy and afflicted. It means going out of ourselves in order to enter into efficacious solidarity with our neighbor in need. Mercy, as an expression of love for our brothers and sisters, must reach out to every form of need, every type of misery, both material and spiritual. For, in the Christian praxis of love, it is the poor in their material misery and sinners in their spiritual misery, who are the privileged recipients of mercy, and hence evangelization." (p. 51)

Jones (*The Christ of the Mount*) comments that, "mercy without righteousness is mushy. To be merciful toward the failings and sins of others without a moral protest at the heart of the mercy ends in looseness and libertinism. Either righteousness or mercy taken alone smells bad, but put together there is a breath of heavenly scent upon them." (p. 74)

Lloyd-Jones (*Sermon on the Mount*) comments that, "if you are merciful, you have mercy in this way. You already have it, but you will have it every time you sin, because when you realize what you have done you will come back to God and say, 'Have mercy upon me, O God.' But remember this. If, when you sin, you see it and in repentance go to God, and there on your knees immediately realize that you are not forgiving somebody else, you will have no confidence in your prayers; you will despise yourself… It is a solemn serious, and, in a sense, terrible thing to say that you cannot be truly forgiven unless there is a forgiving spirit in you. For the operation of the grace of God is such, that when it comes into our hearts with forgiveness it makes us merciful." (p. 104)

Matthew 5:8 - Blessed are the pure in heart, for they will see God.

BLESSED (*makarios*) – See the description for blessed in the Matthew 5:3. *The Amplified Bible* describes *makarios* as "happy, spiritually prosperous (with life-joy and satisfaction in God's favor and salvation, regardless of their outward conditions."

PURE (*batharismos*) – In Matthew 5:8, *batharismos* is a nominative masculine plural that means "pure ones." Vine (*Expository Dictionary of N.T. Words*) defines *batharismos* as "free from impure admixture, without blemish, spotless." (p. 194) Kittle (*Theological Dictionary of the N.T*) describes *batharismos* as "physical, religious, and moral cleanness or purity in such senses as clean, free from stains or shame, and free from adulteration." (p. 381)

Stott (*SOM*) comments that purity of heart "requires heart-righteousness rather than mere rule-righteousness." (p. 49)

Jordon (*Sermon on the Mount*) writes that, "the new heart that He gives will be a pure one, like His. It will make a clear, decisive, complete break with sin in all its many forms. This break will be followed, not by a wistful longing or even a toleration of the old life, but by an utter abhorrence of it." (p. 32)

HEART (*kardia*) – Vine defines *kardia* as "the chief organ of the physical life… By an easy transition the word came to stand for man's entire mental and moral activity, both the rational and emotional elements. In other words, the heart is used figuratively for the hidden springs of the personal life." (p. 206-207)

Bonhoeffer (*The Cost of Discipleship*) states that, "the pure heart is pure alike of good and evil, it belongs exclusively to Christ and looks only to Him who goes on before. Only they will see God, who in this life have looked solely unto Christ, the Son of God. For then their hearts are free from all defiling fantasies and are not distracted by conflicting desires and intentions." (p. 126)

SEE (*opsomai*) – In Matthew 5:8, *opsomai* is a third person plural future indicative verb that means the future fact of seeing god. Vine comments that *opsomai* is the future tense of *horao* that means "bodily vision." Vine further states that *opsomai* "indicates the direction of the thought to the object seen… *horao* gives prominence to the discerning mind." (p. 337) Kittle defines *horao* as "to look, to see, to experience, to perceive, to take note, to take care." (p. 706)

Jones (*The Christ of the Mount*) suggests that, "the seeing of God is not through self-emptying alone, but the self-emptying is in order to a filling with the positive qualities of vicarious suffering, of meekness, of hunger and thirst after righteousness, of a tender mercy and a purity in the heart. All these qualities fit one for finer relationships with man, so that God is seen, not apart from life, but in the midst of human relationships." (p. 75)

Lloyd-Jones (*Sermon on the Mount*) comments that, "there is a vision possible to the eye of faith that no one else has. But there is a seeing also in the sense of knowing Him, a sense of feeling He is near, and enjoying His presence." (p. 114)

GOD (*theos*) – Vine comments that *theos* "in the polytheism of the Greeks, denotes a god or deity… Hence the word was appropriated by Jews and retained by Christians to denote the one true God. In the Sept. *theos* translates (with few exceptions) the Hebrew words *Elohim* and *Jehovah*, the former indicating His power and pre-eminence, the later His unoriginated, unmutable, eternal and self-sustaining existence." (p. 160)

Matthew 5:9 - Blessed are the peacemakers, for they will be called sons of God.

BLESSED (*makarios*) – See the description of blessed in the Matthew 5:3. *The Amplified Bible* describes *makarios* as "happy, spiritually prospersous (with life-joy and satisfaction in God's favor and salvation, regardless of their outward conditions)."

PEACEMAKERS (*eirenopoios*) – In Matthew 5:9, *eirenopoios* is a nominative masculine plural meaning "peacemakers and maintainers." *Eirenopoios* comes from the root *eirene* that Kittle (*Theological Dictionary of the N.T.*) describes as "a state, not a relationship or attitude. It is the opposite of *polemos* ('war'). It is linked with treaties of peace or the conclusion of peace. It is also the opposite of disturbance. In a negative sense, it may denote a peaceful attitude, i.e.., the absence of hostile feelings." (p. 207) Kittle further defines *eirenopoios* as "one who makes peace." (p. 210)

Barclay (*GOM*, Vol. 1) states that, "in Greek the word (for peace) is *eirene*, and in the Hebrew it is *shalom*. In Hebrew peace always means everything which makes for a man's highest good… In the Bible peace means not only freedom from all trouble; it means enjoyment of all good." (p. 108)

Driver (*Kingdom Citizens*) writes that, "Peace in this beatitude should be understood in its biblical Hebrew meaning, *shalom*. We should remember that Jesus and his disciples were Jews in their way of thinking and doing. *Shalom* was a fundamental concept among the Hebrew people. It meant well-being, or health, or salvation in its fullest sense, material as well a whole (healed) relationships among persons, as well as between persons and God." (p. 68)

Lloyd-Jones (*Sermon on the Mount*) comments that, "as peacemakers, we should be endeavoring to diffuse peace wherever we are. We do this by being selfless, by being lovable, by being approachable and by not standing on our own dignity." (p. 125)

PEACE IN THE BIBLE

The following information is taken from J.D. Douglas (ed.), *New Bible Dictionary*, 1970, Grand Rapids, MI: Eerdmans, p. 956

I. Old Testament concepts of peace – *shalom* – "completeness, soundness, well-being"

    A.   Prayer for the welfare of others – Gen. 43:27, Ex. 4:18, Jdg. 19:20
    B.   Harmony between people – Jos. 9:15, I Kings 5:12
    C.   Seeking the good of a city or country – Ps. 122:6, Jer. 29:7
    D.   Material prosperity – Ps. 73:3
    E.   Physical safety – Ps. 4:8
    F.   Spiritual well-being – Ps. 85:10, Is. 48:18 & 22, Is. 57:19-21

G. Messianic age of peace – Is. 2:2-4, Is. 11:1-9, Hg. 2:7-9

H. Prince of peace – Is. 9:6, Jer. 33:15, Ezek. 34:23, Mic. 5:5, Zech. 9:9

II. New Testament concepts of peace – *eirene* – "peace, harmony"

A. Peace has come in Christ – Lk. 1:79, 2:14, 29

B. Peace is bestowed through Christ – Mk. 5:34, Lk. 7:50, Jn. 20:19, 21, 26

C. His disciples are messengers of peace – Lk. 5:5, Acts 10:36

Additional passages in the N.T. where *eirene* is used – Matt. 10:34; Lk. 1:79, 2:14, 12:51; Jn. 14:27, 16:33; Rom. 5:1, 10:15, 12:18, 14:19, 16:20; I Cor. 14:33; Gal. 5:22; Eph. 2:14, 4:3; Phil. 4:7,9; col. 3:15; II Tim. 2:22; Heb. 12:14; Jas. 3:18.

CALLED (*kaleo*) – In Matthew 5:9, *kaleo* is a third person plural future passive indicative verb that means the future fact of being called Sons of God. Kittle defines *kaleo* as "'to call,' but often has a special nuance of divine calling or vocation." (p. 394)

SONS (*huios*) – In Matthew 5:9, *huios* is a nominative (noun) plural. Vine (*Expository Dictionary of N.T. Words*) defines *huios* as "primarily signifies the relation of offspring to parent (see John 9:18-20; Gal. 4:30). It is often used metaphorically of prominent moral characteristics… Jesus uses *huios* in a very significant way, as in Matt. 5:9…and Matt. 5:44-45… The disciples were to do these things, not in order that they might become children of God, but that, being children… they make the fact manifest in their character…" (p. 47)

Bonhoeffer (*The Cost of Discipleship*) states that, "the peacemakers will carry the cross with their Lord, for it was on the cross that peace was made. Now that they are partners in Christ's work of reconciliation, they are called sons of God as he is the Son of God." (p. 126-127)

Barclay (*GOM*, Vol. 1) comments that, "the Greek more literally is that the peacemakers will be called the sons (*huioi*) of God. This is a typical Hebrew way of expression. Hebrew is not rich in adjectives, and often when a Hebrew wishes to describe something, it uses, not an adjective, but the phrase son of… plus an abstract noun. Hence a man may be called a son of peace instead of a peaceful man… what it means is: Blessed are the peace-makers, for they shall be doing a God-life work. The man who makes peace is engaged on the very work which the God of peace is doing (Rom. 15:33; II Cor. 13:11; I Thes. 5:23; Heb. 13:20)." (p. 109)

GOD (*theos*) – See the description of God in the Matthew 5:8. Vine comments that *theos* denotes "the one true God."

Matthew 5:10-12 - Blessed are those who are persecuted because of righteousness, for theirs is the kingdom of heaven. Blessed are you when people insult you, persecute you and falsely say all kinds of evil against you because of me. Rejoice and be glad, because great is your reward in heaven, for in the same way they persecuted the prophets who were born before you.

BLESSED (*makarios*) – See description for blessed in Matthew 5:3. *The Amplified Bible* describes *makarios* as "happy, spiritually prosperous (with life-joy and satisfaction in God's favor and salvation, regardless of their outward conditions)."

PERSECUTED (*dioko*) – In Matthew 5:10, *dioko* is a nominative plural masculine perfect passive participle meaning "having been persecuted." Machen (*N.T. Greek*) states that, "the Greek perfect tense denotes the present state resultant upon a past action." (p. 187) Vine (*Expository Dictionary of N.T. Words*) defines *dioko* as "(a) to put to flight, drive away, (b) to pursue, whence the meaning to persecute, Matt. 5:10-12, 44…" (p. 178) Kittle (*Theological Dictionary of the N.T.*) defines *dioko* as "to follow zealously' as (a) 'to attach oneself to a person' or (b) 'to pursue or promote a cause.'" (p. 177)

RIGHTEOUSNESS (*dikaiosune*) – See the descriptions of righteousness in the Matthew 5:6. In Matthew 5:10, *dikaiosune* is an accusative singular (direct object) of the adverb *eneka* ("for the sake of") meaning "for the sake of righteousness."

Boise (*The Sermon on the Mount*) states that, "first, persecution is evidence that the believer is united to Jesus Christ. Jesus said, 'if ye were of this world, the world would love its own; but because ye are not of the world, but I have chosen you out of the world, therefore the world hateth you.' (John 15:19)… Second, if we are persecuted for righteousness sake, we can be certain that the Holy Spirit has been at work in our hearts, turning us from our sin and sinful ways to Christ's way, and is making progress in molding us into His sinless image." (p. 61)

Briscoe (*Tough Truths for Today's Living*) comments that, "persecution is coming upon us, make no mistake on that score. Our identification with Christ automatically means alienation from Satan. Our identification with truth automatically means alienation from lies. And alienation is a close relative of persecution." (p. 48)

Bonhoeffer (*The Cost of Discipleship*) concludes that, "the world will be offended at them, and so the disciples will be persecuted for righteousness sake. Not recognition is the reward they get from the world for their message and their works." (p. 127)

KINGDOM OF HEAVEN (*basileia*) – See the description of the kingdom of heaven in Matthew 5:3.

INSULT (*oneidizo*) – In Matthew 5:11, *oneidizo* is a third person plural first aorist subjective that means "when they reproach you." Machen states that the aorist subjective "refers to the action without saying anything about its continuance or repetition…" (p. 131) Kittle defines *oneidizo* as "'to revile,' and it means 'disgrace,' 'abuse,' or 'object of disgrace or shame.'" (p. 693)

PERSECUTE (*dioko*) – See the description of persecute above. *The Analytical Greek Lexicon* defines *dioko* as "to pursue with malignity, persecute…" (p. 104)

SAY ALL EVIL (*poneros*) – In Matthew 5:11, *poneros* is an accusative (direct object) singular of the subjunctive *eipon* ("to say") that means literally "to speak all evil against you." Kittle states that *poneros* comes from a group of words denoting "poverty or need." He further defines *poneros* as meaning "full of trouble," "useless," "wrong," "harmful," "contrary," and "morally bad," "evil." (p. 912)

REJOICE (*chairo*) – In Matthew 5:12, *chairo* is a second person plural present imperative that means that ongoing rejoicing is commanded of disciples by Christ. Kittle defines *chairo* as "to rejoice, to be merry… *Chaire* serves as a morning greeting. It is above all a greeting to the gods and is a stereotyped ending to hymns." (p. 1299)

GLAD (*agalliamai*) – In Matthew 5:12, *agalliamai* is second person plural present middle imperative that means that ongoing gladness is commanded of disciples by Christ. Kittle defines *agalliamai* as "'to adorn…' 'to plume oneself, expressing joyful pride… the main use is for exalting in God's acts (Rev. 19:7)." (p. 4)

Barclay (*GOM*, Vol. 1) comments that, "the word for be glad is from the verb *agalliasthai* which has been derived from two Greek words which mean to leap exceedingly." (p. 116)

REWARD (*misthos*) – Vine defines *misthos* as "primarily wages, hire, and then, generally, reward…" (p. 294)

The Beatitudes:
The Process of Inward Renewal

**And when He saw the multitudes,
He went up on the mountain;
and after He sat down, His disciples
came to Him. And opening His mouth
He began to teach them, saying,**

Verse	Spiritual Condition	My Responsibility	God's Response
3	**Blessed** - happy, spiritually prosperous (with life-joy and satisfaction in God's favor and salvation, regardless of their outward conditions). -- *The AMPLIFIED Bible*	**poor in spirit** → poverty stricken, powerless to enrich. --*Vine* utter destitution, which abjectly solicits and lives by alms. --*Vincent* ... to acknowldge our spiritual poverty, indeed our spiritual bankruptcy, before God. --*Stott*	**kingdom of heaven** sovereignty, royal power... the territory or people over whom a king rules. --*Vine* ... we are in the realm of a kingdom which is unlike everything that belongs to this 'present evil world.' --*Lloyd-Jones*
4	"a sense of God's approval founded in righteousness which rests ultimately on love to God." --*Vincent*	**mourn** → grief manifested, too deep for concealment. --*Vincent* those who mourn the loss of their innocence, their righteousness, their self-respect... the sorrow of repentance. --*Stott*	**comforted** a calling to one's side, and so to one's aid. --*Vine* Such mourners who bewail their own sinfulness, will be comforted by the only comfort which can relieve their distress, namely the free forgiveness of God. --*Stott*
5		**meek** → temper of spirit in which we accept His dealings with us as good, and therefore without disputing or resisting... opposite of self-assertiveness and self-interest... --*Vine* the gentleness of strength. --*Robertson*	**inherit the earth** new perspective on our relationship with the earth -- harmony with and stewardship of God's creation. --*Leavenworth*
6		**hunger and thirst for righteousness** → basic life forces passionate hunger and thirst for goodness and holiness. --*Robertson* a desire to be right with God. --*Lloyd-Jones*	**satisfied** to fill or satisfy with food. --*Vine* It is not enough to mourn over past sin; we must also hunger for future righteousness. -- *Stott*

Verse	Spiritual Condition	My Responsibility	God's Response
7	Blessed	**merciful** — it is the outward manifestation of pity; it assumes need on the part of him who receives it, and resources adequate to meet the need on the part of him who shows it. *--Vine*	**mercy** grace takes away the fault and mercy takes away the misery. *--Vincent* we cannot receive the mercy and forgiveness of God unless we repent, and we cannot claim to have repented our sins if we are unmerciful toward the sins of others. *--Lloyd-Jones*
8		**pure in heart** — inward purity... sincerity... free from falsehood. Their very heart - including their thoughts and motives is pure, unmixed with anything devious, ulterior or base. *--Stott*	**see God** Christian people can see God in a sense that nobody else can... in the events of history... But there is a seeing also in the sense of knowing Him, a sense of feeling He is near, and enjoying His presence. *--Lloyd-Jones* See His presence in our lives.
9		**peacemakers** — makers and maintainers of peace *--AMPLIFIED* not only keep the peace, but bring men into harmony with each other. *--Vincent*	**sons of God** the relationship of offspring to parent... their conduct gives evidence of the dignity of their relationship. *--Vine*
10 - 12		**persecuted** — (for righteousness) to put to flight, drive away. *--Vine* 1. revile - verbal attack 2. persecution - physical attack 3. Speak evil - gossip	**kingdom of heaven** same as verse 3

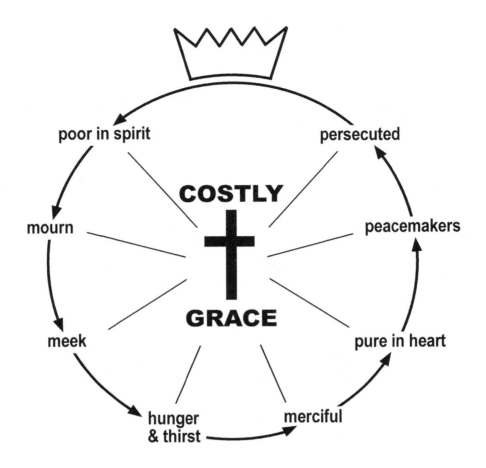

Application (A):

What insights about discipleship have you gained from this chapter?

While praying through this list of insights, ask God which of these you are already applying and which you need to start applying. Try to identify strengths and weaknesses, and prioritize which weaknesses God wants you to work on.

Identify the top priority issue that God wants you to work on and formulate a study/application plan to allow God to graciously begin his transforming work in your heart. What is God's top priority issue and how are you going to cooperate with him in this?

Is there a mentor or accountability partner who can help you by giving wise counsel, praying, encouraging, holding you accountable, etc.? Who is it and how/when will you contact him/her?

CHAPTER 4

Matthew 5:13-16 – Salt and Light

5:13 Ye are the salt of the earth: but if the salt have lost his savour, wherewith shall it be salted? it is thenceforth good for nothing, but to be cast out, and to be trodden under foot of men. 14 Ye are the light of the world. A city that is set on an hill cannot be hid. 15 Neither do men light a candle, and put it under a bushel, but on a candlestick; and it giveth light unto all that are in the house. 16 Let your light so shine before men, that they may see your good works, and glorify your Father which is in heaven. (KJV)

Introduction (I): Go to biblegateway.com for additional translations and paraphrases.

(NIV) 5:13 "You are the salt of the earth. But if the salt loses its saltiness, how can it be made salty again? It is no longer good for anything, except to be thrown out and trampled underfoot. 14 "You are the light of the world. A town built on a hill cannot be hidden. 15 Neither do people light a lamp and put it under a bowl. Instead they put it on its stand, and it gives light to everyone in the house. 16 In the same way, let your light shine before others, that they may see your good deeds and glorify your Father in heaven.

(NASB) 5:13 "You are the salt of the earth; but if the salt has become tasteless, how can it be made salty again? It is no longer good for anything, except to be thrown out and trampled under foot by men. 14 "You are the light of the world. A city set on a hill cannot be hidden; 15 nor does anyone light a lamp and put it under a basket, but on the lampstand, and it gives light to all who are in the house. 16 Let your light shine before men in such a way that they may see your good works, and glorify your Father who is in heaven.

(Message) [5:13] "Let me tell you why you are here. You're here to be salt-seasoning that brings out the God-flavors of this earth. If you lose your saltiness, how will people taste godliness? You've lost your usefulness and will end up in the garbage. [14-16] "Here's another way to put it: You're here to be light, bringing out the God-colors in the world. God is not a secret to be kept. We're going public with this, as public as a city on a hill. If I make you light-bearers, you don't think I'm going to hide you under a bucket, do you? I'm putting you on a light stand. Now that I've put you there on a hilltop, on a light stand—shine! Keep open house; be generous with your lives. By opening up to others, you'll prompt people to open up with God, this generous Father in heaven.

Discovery (D): Study Guide for Matthew 5:13-16 – Salt and Light

Read the passage in the KJV and respond to the following questions:

1. (5:13) What are the properties of "salt" and how is salt related to the Beatitudes?

2. (5:13) What happens when "salt" loses its looses "savour"?

3. (5:14) What are the properties of "light" and how is light related to the Beatitudes?

4. (5:15) What happens when a "candle ... is put under a bushel"?

5. (5:16) How are Jesus' disciples suppose to live their lives as "salt" and light" and what is the result when they do?

6. (5:13-16) What is your interpretation and application of this passage?

Explanation (E):

5:13 **SALT** (*halas*) – Vine (*Expository Dictionary of N.T. Words*) writes that, "being possessed of purifying, perpetuating and antiseptic qualities, salt became emblematic of fidelity and friendship among eastern nations… in the Lord's teaching it is also a symbol of that spiritual health and vigor essential to Christian virtue and counteractive of corruption that is in the world…" (p. 315). In the context of Matthew 5:13, *halas* is a nominative (direct object) of the verb *eime* ("to be") that is a second person plural present indicative. This phrase means that the disciples are salt of the earth on an ongoing, daily basis.

LOSES IT SALTINESS (*moraino*) – In Matthew 5:13, *moraino* is a third person singular first aorist passive subjunctive verb meaning the loss of saltiness at a point in time. Vine says of *moraino* that it means "primarily, to be foolish, is used of salt that has lost its savor…" (p. 323) Kittle (*Theological Dictionary of the N.T.*) writes that, "*moro* and cognates denote deficiency, e.g., physical sloth, but more especially mental dullness. We find such varied uses as for insipid foods, animals that are sluggish in winter, or people suffering from fatigue. With a human reference, the main use is psychological. What is meant is a weakness of understanding or judgment, sometimes through stupidity, sometimes through confusion, but always demanding censure." (p. 620)

BE MADE SALTY (halizo) – In Matthew 5:13, *halizo* is a third person singular passive future verb meaning "to be made salty again." Vine defines *halizo* as "to sprinkle or to season with salt." (p. 316)

GOOD (*ischuo*) – In Matthew 5:13, *ischuo* is a third person singular present indicative verb that means the fact of the ongoing quality of losing its good effects. Kittle says that "the group *ischy*-has the sense of 'ability,' 'capacity,' 'power,' or 'strength.' It overlaps with a *dyna*-group, but with greater stress on the power implied." (p. 378)

THROWN OUT (*ballo*) – In Matthew 5:13, *ballo* is a first aorist passive participle meaning action at a point in time prior to the salt loosing its saltiness. Machen (*N.T. Greek*) states that, "the aorist participle denotes action prior to the action denoted by the leading verb…" (p. 116-117) Vine defines *ballo* as "to throw, hurl, in contrast to striking…" (p. 171)

TRAMPLED BY (*katapateo*) – In Matthew 5:13, *katapateo* is a present passive infinitive verb that means the ongoing or repeated action of trampling under foot.

Barclay (*GOM*, Vol. 1) comments that, "the essential point remains whatever the picture, and it is a point which the New Testament makes and remakes again and again – uselessness invites disaster. If a Christian is not fulfilling his purpose as a Christian, then he is on the way to disaster. We are meant to be salt of the earth, and if we do not bring to life the purity, the antiseptic power, the radiance we ought, then we invite disaster." (p. 121)

Jordan (*Sermon the Mount*) states that, "He called them salt for but one purpose—to warn them that they can loose their power to salt. When this happens, men will no longer bother to persecute Christians. They'll do something even worse; they'll dump them out and go on about their business." (p. 141)

Bonhoeffer (*The Cost of Discipleship*) writes that, "the judgment which always hangs over the disciple community, whose mission is to save the world, but which, if it ceases to live up to that mission, is itself irretrievably lost. The call of Jesus Christ means either that we are the salt of the earth, or else we are annihilated; either we follow the call or we are crushed beneath it." (p. 131)

5:14 **LIGHT** (*phos*) – Vine defines *phos* as "akin to *phao*, to give light (from roots *pha-* and *phan-*), expressing light as seen by the eye, and metaphorically, as reaching the mind, whence *phaino*, to make to appear, *phaneros*, evident…" (p. 340) In the context of Matthew 5:14, *phos* is a nominative (direct object) of the verb *eime* ("to be") that is a second person plural present indicative meaning that the disciples are light to the world on an ongoing, daily basis.

HIDDEN (*krupto*) – In Matthew 5:14, *krupto* is a second aorist passive meaning completed action at a point in time in the past. Vine defines *krupto* as "to cover, conceal, keep secret…" (p. 218)

5:16 **SHINE** (*lampo*) – In Matthew 5:16, *lampo* is a third person singular first aorist imperative verb that means that we are commanded to shine at a point in time. Vine defines *lampo* as "to shine as a torch…" (p. 22)

GOOD (*kalos*) – Vine defines *kalos* as "that which is intrinsically good, and so, goodly, fair, beautiful, as (a) that which is well adapted to its circumstances or ends.. (b) that which is ethically good, right, noble, honorable…" (p. 164) Kittle writes that "all of these senses may be brought together under the idea of 'what is ordered or sound,' and with this basic sense, *kalos* is a key term in Greek thought." (p. 402)

DEEDS (*ergon*) – Kittle defines *ergon* as "action or active zeal. They occur in relation to all kinds of work, working with various materials, building and technical and cultural activity. They also denote work as a social or ethical task." (p. 251) In the context of Matthew 5:16, *aklos* and *ergon* are the direct object of the verb *horao* ("to see") that is a third person plural second aorist subjunctive meaning that the disciples are to be seen by men as demonstrating good at a point in time.

PRAISE (*doxazo*) – In Matthew 5:16, *doxazo* is a third person plural first aorist active subjunctive verb that means that the disciples good deeds cause men to praise God at a point in time. Vine defines *doxazo* as "to suppose (from *doxa*, an opinion); in the N.T. (a) to magnify, extol, praise… especially of glorifying God, i.e., ascribing honor to Him, acknowledging Him as to His being, attributes and acts… (b) to do honor to, to make glorious…" (p. 152)

Stott (*SOM*) comments that, "the function of salt is largely negative: it prevents decay. The function of light is positive; it illumines the darkness. So Jesus calls his disciples to exert a double influence on the secular community, a negative influence by arresting its decay and a positive influence by bringing light into its darkness. For it is one thing to stop the spread of evil; it is another to promote the spread of truth, beauty, and goodness." (p. 64-65)

Application (A):

What insights about discipleship have you gained from this chapter?

While praying through this list of insights, ask God which of these you are already applying and which you need to start applying. Try to identify strengths and weaknesses, and prioritize which weaknesses God wants you to work on.

Identify the top priority issue that God wants you to work on and formulate a study/application plan to allow God to graciously begin his transforming work in your heart. What is God's top priority issue and how are you going to cooperate with him in this?

Is there a mentor or accountability partner who can help you by giving wise counsel, praying, encouraging, holding you accountable, etc.? Who is it and how/when will you contact him/her?

CHAPTER 5

Matthew 5:17-20 – Fulfillment of the Law

5:17 Think not that I am come to destroy the law, or the prophets: I am not come to destroy, but to fulfill. 18 For verily I say unto you, Till heaven and earth pass, one jot or one tittle shall in no wise pass from the law, till all be fulfilled. 19 Whosoever therefore shall break one of these least commandments, and shall teach men so, he shall be called the least in the kingdom of heaven: but whosoever shall do and teach them, the same shall be called great in the kingdom of heaven. 20 For I say unto you, That except your righteousness shall exceed the righteousness of the scribes and Pharisees, ye shall in no case enter into the kingdom of heaven. (KJV)

Introduction (I): Go to biblegateway.com for additional translations and paraphrases.

(NIV) 5:17 "Do not think that I have come to abolish the Law or the Prophets; I have not come to abolish them but to fulfill them. 18 For truly I tell you, until heaven and earth disappear, not the smallest letter, not the least stroke of a pen, will by any means disappear from the Law until everything is accomplished. 19 Therefore anyone who sets aside one of the least of these commands and teaches others accordingly will be called least in the kingdom of heaven, but whoever practices and teaches these commands will be called great in the kingdom of heaven. 20 For I tell you that unless your righteousness surpasses that of the Pharisees and the teachers of the law, you will certainly not enter the kingdom of heaven.

(NASB) 5:17 "Do not think that I have come to abolish the Law or the Prophets; I have not come to abolish them but to fulfill them. 18 For truly I tell you, until heaven and earth disappear, not the smallest letter, not the least stroke of a pen, will by any means disappear from the Law until everything is accomplished. [19] Therefore anyone who sets aside one of the least of these commands and teaches others accordingly will be called least in the kingdom of heaven, but whoever practices and teaches these commands will be called great in the kingdom of heaven. [20] For I tell you that unless your righteousness surpasses that of the Pharisees and the teachers of the law, you will certainly not enter the kingdom of heaven.

(Message) [5:17-18] "Don't suppose for a minute that I have come to demolish the Scriptures—either God's Law or the Prophets. I'm not here to demolish but to complete. I am going to put it all together, pull it all together in a vast panorama. God's Law is more real and lasting than the stars in the sky and the ground at your feet. Long after stars burn out and earth wears out, God's Law will be alive and working. [19-20] "Trivialize even the smallest item in God's Law and you will only have trivialized yourself. But take it seriously, show the way for others, and you will find honor in the kingdom. Unless you do far better than the Pharisees in the matters of right living, you won't know the first thing about entering the kingdom.

Discovery (D): Study Guide for Matthew 5:17-20 – Fulfillment of the Law

Read the passage in the KJV and respond to the following questions:

1. (5:17) What is meant by the "law" or the "prophets" and why are they important?

2. (5:17) What does "destroy" and "fulfill" mean?

3. (5:18-19) What is the importance of the fulfillment of the law and what will happen to those who "break one of these least commandments"?

4. (5:19) What is the relationship between knowing, teaching, and doing the law?

5. (5:20) What does it mean to "exceed the righteousness of the scribes and Pharisees" and why is this important?

6. (5:17-20) What is your interpretation and application of this passage?

Explanation (E):

5:17 **ABOLISH** (*kataluo*) – In Matthew 5:17, *kataluo* is an aroist first active infinitive (verbal noun) meaning "to abolish" at a point in time. Vine (*Expository Dictionary of N.T. Words*) defines *kataluo* as "*kata*, down, intensive, and… to destroy utterly, to overthrow completely…" (p. 302)

LAW OR THE PROPHETS (*nomos/prophetes*) – Vine defines law as "akin to *nemo*, to divide out, distribute, primarily meant that which is assigned; hence, usage, custom, and then, law, as prescribed by custom, or by statue; the word *ethos*, custom, was retained for unwritten law, while *nomos* became the established name for the law as decreed by a state and set up as the standard for the administration of justice." (p. 313) Vine defines *prophetes* as "one who speaks forth openly... a proclaimer of the divine message, denoted among the Greeks as an interpreter of the oracles of the gods." (p. 222)

Barclay (*SOM*, Vol. 1) comments that, "the Jews used the expression The Law in four different ways. (I) They used it to mean the Ten Commandments. (II) They used it to mean the first five books of the Bible (Pentatuch)... (III) They used the phrase The Law and the prophets to mean the whole of the Scripture... (IV) They used it to mean the Oral or the Scribal Law." (p. 127)

FULFILL (*pleroo*) – In Matthew 5:17, *pleroo* is an aorist active infinitive (verbal noun) meaning "to fulfill" at a point in time. Vine defines *pleroo* as "(1) to fill... (2) to fulfill, complete..." (p. 135)

Chambers (*Studies in the Sermon on the Mount*) comments that, "our Lord places Himself as the exact meaning and fulfillment of all Old Testament prophecies... Our Lord goes behind the old law to the disposition. Everything He teaches is impossible unless He can put into us His spirit and remake us from within. The Sermon on the Mount is quite unlike the Ten Commandments in the sense of its being absolutely unworkable unless Jesus Christ can remake us." (p. 19)

TRUTH (*amen*) – Vine defines *amen* as "the translation of a Hebrew word 'truth,' is usually translated 'verily' in the four Gospels..." (p. 185) Vine further comments that "its meaning may be seen in such passages as Deut. 7:9, 'the faithful (the *amen*) God,' Isa. 49:7, 'Jehovah that is faithful,' 65:16, 'the God of truth'... and if God is faithful His testimonies and precepts are sure (*amen*), Ps. 19:7, 111:7, as are also His warnings, Hos. 5:9, and promises, Isa. 33:16, 55:3... This '*amen*' said by God 'it is and shall be so,' and by men, 'so let it be.'" (p. 53) *Amen* relates to the verb *lego* ("to speak") that is a first person singular present active subjunctive meaning on-going action.

5:18 **SMALLEST LETTER** – Barclay (*GOM*, Vol. 1) comments that, "the smallest letter - the letter which the Authorized Version calls the jot - was the Hebrew letter *idoh*. In form it was like an apostrophe; not even a letter not much bigger than a dot was to pass away. The smallest part of the letter—what the Authorized Version calls the tittle—is what we call the serif, the little projecting part of the foot of the letter, the little line at each side of the foot of, for example, the letter I. Jesus seems to lay it down that the law is so sacred that not the smallest detail of it will ever pass away." (p. 127)

DISAPPEAR (*parerchomai*) – In Matthew 5:18, *parerchomai* is a third person singular aorist second subjunctive verb that means "to pass away" at a point in time. Vine defines *parerchomai* as "from *para*, by, *erchomai*, to come or to, denotes (I), literally, to pass, pass by… (II), metaphorically, (a) to pass away, to perish, Matt. 5:18… (b) to pass by, disregard, neglect, pass over, Luke 11:42…" (p. 164)

ACCOMPLISHED (*ginomai*) – In Matthew 5:18, *ginomai* is a third person singular aorist second subjunctive verb that means "to complete" at a point in time. Vine defines *ginomai* as "to become, to take place, is rendered 'fulfilled' in the A.V. of Matt. 5:18…" (p. 136)

5:19 BREAKS (*luo*) – In Matthew 5:19, *luo* is a third person singular aorist first active subjunctive verb that means "to break" at a point in time. Vine defines *luo* as "to loosen especially by way of a deliverance, sometimes has the meaning of breaking, destructively, e.g., of breaking commandments, not only infringing them, but loosing the force of them, rendering them not binding, Matt. 5:19…" (p 147)

TEACHES (*didasko*) – In Matthew 5:19, *didasko* is third person singular aorist first active subjunctive that means "to teach" at a point in time. *Didasko* means to "give instruction" or to explain the meaning of something.

PRACTICES (*poieo*) – In Matthew 5:19, *poieo* is third person singular aorist first active subjunctive that means "to do" at a point in time. Vine defines *poieo* as "(a) to make, (b) to do, i.e., to adopt a way of expressing by act of the thoughts and feelings." (p. 330)

5:20 RIGHTEOUSNESS (*dikaiosume*) – See Matthew 5:6 for description of righteousness. *Dikaiosume* means "right relationship" and "right action."

SURPASSES (*perisseuo*) – In Matthew 5:20, *perisseuo* is a third person singular aorist first subjunctive verb that means "to exceed" at a point in time. Vine defines *perisseuo* as "to be over and above, over a certain number of measure, to abound, exceed, is translated exceed in Matt. 5:20…" (p. 54)

PHARISEES AND TEACHERS (*pharisaios/grammateus*) – Vine defines *pharisaios* as "from the Aramaic word *peras* (found in Deut. 5:28), signifying to separate, owing to a different manner of life from that of the general public." (p. 181) Vine defines *grammateus* as "from *gramma*, a writing, denotes a scribe, a man of letters, a teacher of the law; the scribes are mentioned frequently in the Synoptic Gospels, especially in connection with the Pharisees, with whom they virtually formed one party.'" (p. 328)

Stott (*SOM*) suggests that, "what the scribes and Pharisees were doing, in order to make obedience more readily attainable, was to restrict the commandments and extend the permissions of the law. They made the laws demands less demanding and the law's permissions more permissive. What Jesus did was to reverse both tendencies. He insisted instead that the full implications of God's commandments must be accepted without imposing any artificial limits, whereas the limits which God had set to his permissions must also be accepted and not arbitrarily increased." (p. 79)

Application (A):

What insights about discipleship have you gained from this chapter?

While praying through this list of insights, ask God which of these you are already applying and which you need to start applying. Try to identify strengths and weaknesses, and prioritize which weaknesses God wants you to work on.

Identify the top priority issue that God wants you to work on and formulate a study/application plan to allow God to graciously begin his transforming work in your heart. What is God's top priority issue and how are you going to cooperate with him in this?

Is there a mentor or accountability partner who can help you by giving wise counsel, praying, encouraging, holding you accountable, etc.? Who is it and how/when will you contact him/her?

CHAPTER 6

Matthew 5:21-26 – Murder

5:21 Ye have heard that it was said of them of old time, Thou shalt not kill; an whosoever shall kill shall be in danger of the judgment: **22** But I say unto you, That whosoever is angry with his brother without a cause shall be in danger of the judgment: and whosoever shall say to his brother, Raca, shall be in danger of the council: but whosoever shall say, Thou fool, shall be in danger of hell fire. **23** Therefore if thou bring thy gift to the altar, and there rememberest that thy brother hath ought against thee; **24** Leave there thy gift before the altar, and go thy way; first be reconciled to thy brother, and then come and offer thy gift. **25** Agree with thine adversary quickly, whiles thou art in the way with him; lest at any time the adversary deliver thee to the judge, and the judge deliver thee to the officer, and thou be cast into prison. **26** Verily I say unto thee, Thou shalt by no means come out thence, till thou hast paid the uttermost farthing. (KJV)

Introduction (I):   Go to biblegateway.com for additional translations and paraphrases.

(NIV)   **5:21** "You have heard that it was said to the people long ago, 'You shall not murder, and anyone who murders will be subject to judgment.' **22** But I tell you that anyone who is angry with a brother or sister will be subject to judgment. Again, anyone who says to a brother or sister, 'Raca,' is answerable to the court. And anyone who says, 'You fool!' will be in danger of the fire of hell. **23** "Therefore, if you are offering your gift at the altar and there remember that your brother or sister has something against you, **24** leave your gift there in front of the altar. First go and be reconciled to them; then come and offer your gift. **25** "Settle matters quickly with your adversary who is taking you to court. Do it while you are still together on the way, or your adversary may hand you over to the judge, and the judge may hand you over to the officer, and you may be thrown into prison. [26] Truly I tell you, you will not get out until you have paid the last penny.

(NASB) [5:21] "You have heard that the ancients were told, 'YOU SHALL NOT COMMIT MURDER' and 'Whoever commits murder shall be liable to the court.' [22] But I say to you that everyone who is angry with his brother shall be guilty before the court; and whoever says to his brother, ' You good-for-nothing,' shall be guilty before the supreme court; and whoever says, 'You fool,' shall be guilty enough to go into the fiery hell. [23] Therefore if you are presenting your offering at the altar, and there remember that your brother has something against you, [24] leave your offering there before the altar and go; first be reconciled to your brother, and then come and present your offering. [25] Make friends quickly with your opponent at law while you are with him on the way, so that your opponent may not hand you over to the judge, and the judge to the officer, and you be thrown into prison. [26] Truly I say to you, you will not come out of there until you have paid up the last cent.

(Message) [5:21-22] "You're familiar with the command to the ancients, 'Do not murder.' I'm telling you that anyone who is so much as angry with a brother or sister is guilty of murder. Carelessly call a brother 'idiot!' and you just might find yourself hauled into court. Thoughtlessly yell 'stupid!' at a sister and you are on the brink of hellfire. The simple moral fact is that words kill. [23-24] "This is how I want you to conduct yourself in these matters. If you enter your place of worship and, about to make an offering, you suddenly remember a grudge a friend has against you, abandon your offering, leave immediately, go to this friend and make things right. Then and only then, come back and work things out with God. [25-26] "Or say you're out on the street and an old enemy accosts you. Don't lose a minute. Make the first move; make things right with him. After all, if you leave the first move to him, knowing his track record, you're likely to end up in court, maybe even jail. If that happens, you won't get out without a stiff fine.

Discovery (D): Study Guide For Matthew 5:21-26 – Murder

Read the passage in the KJV and respond to the following questions (note that each of the next six Study Guide passages include the phrases, "Ye have heard that… But I say unto you…"):

1. (5:21) What does "Thou shalt not kill…" mean? (Look up at least three other passages that use this word or phrase)

2. (5:21) What does "danger of the judgment" mean? (Look up at least three other passages that use this word or phrase)

3. (5:22) What does "angry… without a cause" mean? (Look up at least three other passages that use this word or phrase)

4. (5:22) What does "Raca" mean?

5. (5:22) What does "Thou fool" mean? (Look up at least three other passages that use this word or phrase)

6. (5:22) What is the sequence and severity of judgment associated with anger, Raca, and fool in this verse?

7. (5:24) What does "first be reconciled to thy brother" mean? (Look up at least three other passages that use this word or phrase)

8. (5:24) Why is reconciliation a prerequisite for "then come and offer thy gift"? How does this relate to the Beatitudes and Salt and Light passages (Matthew 5: 3-16)?

9. (5:23-25) What is Jesus teaching his disciples about the relationship of murder, anger, and reconciliation?

10. (5:21-26) What is your interpretation and application of this passage?

Explanation (E):

5:21 **MURDER** (*phoneuo*) – In Matthew 5:21, *phoneuo* is a second person singular future indicative that means the future fact of killing somebody. Vine (*Expository Dictionary of N.T. Words*) defines *phoneuo* as "to murder, akin to *phoneus*, a murderer, is always rendered by the verb to kill…" (p. 290) The statement "do not murder" is taken from the Ten Commandments in Exodus 20:13.

JUDGEMENT (*krisis*) – Vine defines *krisis* as "a separating, then, a decision, judgment, most frequently in the forensic sense, and especially of Devine Judgment." (p. 281) *Krisis* is the object of the future tense verb *eime* ("to be"), thus it means that judgment will come upon those who murder.

5:22 **ANGRY** (*orgizo*) – In Matthew 5:22, *orgizo* is a present passive participle that means "being angry with." Vine defines *orgizo* as "to provoke, to arouse to anger…" (p. 56) Kittle (*Theological Dictionary of the N.T.*) states that, "*orge* is especially oriented to revenge or punishment." (p. 716)

Barclay (*GOM*, Vol. 1) writes that, "in Greek there are two words for anger. There is *thumos*, which was described as being like the flame which comes from dry straw. It is the anger which quickly blazes up and which just as quickly dies down… There is *orge*, which was described as anger become inveterate. It is the long-lived anger; it is the anger of the man who nurses his wrath to keep it warm; it is the anger over which a person broods, and which he will not allow it to die." (p. 138)

RACA (*raka*) – Vine defines *raka* as "a word of utter contempt, signifying empty, intellectually rather than morally, empty-headed… as condemned by Christ, Matthew 5:22; it was worse than being angry, in as much as an outrageous utterance is worse than a feeling unexpressed or somewhat controlled in expression; it does not indicate such a loss of self-control as the world rendered 'fool,' a godless, moral reprobate." (p. 243)

SANHEDRIN (*sunedrion*) – Vine defines *sunedrion* as "a settling together (*sun*, together, *hedra*, a seat), hence (a) any assembly or session of persons deliberating or adjusting... (b) the Sanhedrin, the great council at Jerusalem, consisting of 71 members, namely, prominent members of the families of the high priest, elders, and scribes. The Jews trace the origin of this to Nu. 11:16. The more important causes came up before this tribunal. The Roman rulers of Judea permitted the Sanhedrin to try such cases, and even to pronounce sentence of death, with the condition that such a sentence should be valid only if confirmed by the Roman Procurator." (p. 245)

FOOL (*moros*) – Vine defines *moros* as "dull, sluggish (from a root *muh*, to be silly); hence stupid, foolish; it is used (a) of persons, Matt. 5:22, 'Thou fool'; here the word means morally worthless, a scoundrel, a more serious reproach than '*Raca*'; the latter scorns a man's mind and calls him stupid; *moros* scorns his heart and character; hence the Lord's more severe condemnations; in 7:26..." (p. 114)

FIRE OF HELL (*geenna*) – Vine defines *geenna* as "the Hebrew *Ge-Himon* (the valley of Tophet) and a corresponding Aramaic word; it is found twelve times in the N.T. ... in every instance as uttered by the Lord Himself." (p. 212) Kittle states that *geenna* "acquired a bad reputation because of the sacrifices offered to Moloch there (2 Kings 16:3). Judgment was pronounced on it (Jer. 7:32), and it thus came to be equated with the hell of the last judgment... later it was also used for the place where the wicked are punished in the intermediate state." (p. 113)

5:23 **OFFERING** (*prosphero*) – In Matthew 5:23, *prosphero* is a second person singular active subjunctive that means the ongoing act of "bringing" one's gift to the alter. The object of *prosphero* is the noun *doron* ("gift"). Vine defines *doron* as "akin to *didomi*, to give, is used (a) of gifts presented as an expression of honor, Matt. 2:11; (b) of gifts for the support of the temple and the needs of the poor, Matt. 15:5... (c) of gifts offered to God, Matt. 5:23, 24... (d) of salvation by grace, as the gift of God, Eph. 2:8; (e) of presents for mutual celebration of an occasion, Rev. 11:10." (p. 146)

SOMETHING AGAINST YOU (*kata*) – *Kata* is a preposition meaning "against." Machen (*N.T. Greek*) states that, "prepositions express relationship." (p. 40) In this case, *kata* is the genitive case that indicates separation.

5:24 **LEAVE** (*aphiemi*) – In Matthew 5:24, *aphiemi* is a second person aorist imperative that means action at a point in time as a command. Vine defines *aphiemi* as "*apo*, from, and *hiemi*, to send, hence three chief meanings, (a) to send forth, let go, forgive; (b) to let, suffer, permit; (c) to leave, leave alone, forsake, neglect." (p. 325)

RECONCILED (*diallasso*) – In Matthew 5:24, *diallasso* is a second person singular aorist passive imperative that means being reconciled to another at a point in time in response to a command. Vine describes *diallasso* as "to effect an alteration, to exchange, and hence, to reconcile, in cases of mutual hostility yielding to mutual concession..." (p. 261)

5:25 **SETTLE** (*eunoeo*) – In Matthew 5:25, *eunoeo* is a nominative singular masculine present participle that means on-going agreement. *Eunoeo* is connected with the present tense verb *eime* ("to be"). Vine defines *eunoeo* as "to be well-minded, well-disposed (*eu*, well, *nous*, the mind), is found in Matt. 5:25, 'agree with." (p. 44)

QUICKLY (*tachu*) – Vine describes *tachu* as "the neuter of *tachus*, swift, quick, signifies quickly, Matt. 5:25..." (p. 241)

ADVERSARY (*antidikos*) – Vine describes *antidikos* as "firstly, an opponent in a lawsuit, Matt. 5:25 (twice)... is also used to denote an adversary or an enemy, without reference to legal affairs..." (p. 34)

JUDGE (*krites*) – Vine defines *krites* as "a judge... primarily denotes to separate, select, choose; hence to determine, and so to judge, pronounce judgment." (p. 279-280)

5:26 **PAID** (*apodidomi*) – In Matthew 5:26, *apodidomi* is a second person singular aorist active subjunctive that means payment at a point in time. Vine defines *apodidomi* as "to give back, to render what is due, to pay..." (p. 169)

BARCLAY (*GOM*, Vol. 1) states that, "Jesus forbids for ever the anger that broods, the anger which will not forget, the anger which refuses to be pacified, the anger which seeks revenge." (p. 139)

Jones (*The Christ of the Mount*) comments that, "you will either begin with humility or end with humiliation. The Christian is under obligation to settle the misunderstanding... wronged or having wronged, the Christians must go to all lengths to settle." (p. 144)

Application (A):

What insights about discipleship have you gained from this chapter?

While praying through this list of insights, ask God which of these you are already applying and which you need to start applying. Try to identify strengths and weaknesses, and prioritize which weaknesses God wants you to work on.

Identify the top priority issue that God wants you to work on and formulate a study/application plan to allow God to graciously begin his transforming work in your heart. What is God's top priority issue and how are you going to cooperate with him in this?

Is there a mentor or accountability partner who can help you by giving wise counsel, praying, encouraging, holding you accountable, etc.? Who is it and how/when will you contact him/her?

CHAPTER 7

Matthew 5:27-30 – Adultery

5:27 Ye have heard that it was said by them of old time, Thou shalt not commit adultery: 28 But I say unto you, That whosoever looketh on a woman to lust after her hath committed adultery with her already in his heart. 29 And if thy right eye offend thee, pluck it out, and cast it from thee: for it is profitable for thee that one of thy members should perish, and not that thy whole body should be cast into hell. 30 And if thy right hand offend thee, cut it off, and cast it from thee: for it is profitable for thee that one of thy members should perish, and not that thy whole body should be cast into hell. (KJV)

Introduction (I): Go to biblegateway.com for additional translations and paraphrases.

(NIV) 5:27 "You have heard that it was said, 'You shall not commit adultery.' 28 But I tell you that anyone who looks at a woman lustfully has already committed adultery with her in his heart. 29 If your right eye causes you to stumble, gouge it out and throw it away. It is better for you to lose one part of your body than for your whole body to be thrown into hell. 30 And if your right hand causes you to stumble, cut it off and throw it away. It is better for you to lose one part of your body than for your whole body to go into hell.

(NASB) 5:27 "You have heard that it was said, 'YOU SHALL NOT COMMIT ADULTERY'; 28 but I say to you that everyone who looks at a woman with lust for her has already committed adultery with her in his heart. 29 If your right eye makes you stumble, tear it out and throw it from you; for it is better for you to lose one of the parts of your body, than for your whole body to be thrown into hell. 30 If your right hand makes you stumble, cut it off and throw it from you; for it is better for you to lose one of the parts of your body, than for your whole body to go into hell.

(Message) ⁵:²⁷⁻²⁸ "You know the next commandment pretty well, too: 'Don't go to bed with another's spouse.' But don't think you've preserved your virtue simply by staying out of bed. Your heart can be corrupted by lust even quicker than your body. Those leering looks you think nobody notices—they also corrupt. ²⁹⁻³⁰ "Let's not pretend this is easier than it really is. If you want to live a morally pure life, here's what you have to do: You have to blind your right eye the moment you catch it in a lustful leer. You have to choose to live one-eyed or else be dumped on a moral trash pile. And you have to chop off your right hand the moment you notice it raised threateningly. Better a bloody stump than your entire being discarded for good in the dump.

Discovery (D): Study Guide For Matthew 5:27-30 – Adultery

Read the passage in the KJV and respond to the following questions (note that this is the second of six consecutive Study Guide passages that include the phrases, "Ye have heard that… But I say unto you…"):

1. (5:27) What does "Thou shalt not commit adultery" mean? (Look up at least three other passages that use this word or phrase)

2. (5:28) What does "lust" mean? (Look up at least three other passages that use this word or phrase)

3. (5:28) What does "adultery with her already in his heart" mean? (Look up at least three other passages that use this word or phrase)

4. (5:27-28) What is the relationship between a person's heart attitude and righteous behavior? How does this relate to the Beatitudes and Salt and Light passages (Matthew 5:3-16)?

5. (5:29-30) What does "pluck it out" and "cut it off" mean? (Note that this is figurative language. Jesus does not mean this literally!)

6. (5:29-30) What is the point that Jesus is making in this passage?

7. (5:27-30) What is your interpretation and application of this passage?

Explanation (E):

5:27 HEARD (*hekon*) – Vine (*Expository Dictionary of N.T. Words*) defines *hekon* as "of free will, willingly…." (p. 217) *Hekon* is related to third person singular aorist first passive indicative verb *rheo* ("to speak") that means the disciples have heard what Jesus is saying at a point in time in the past.

ADULTERY (*moicheuo*) – In Matthew 5:27, *moicheuo* is a second person singular future indicative that means the prohibition against a future act of adultery. Kittle (*Theological Dicionary of the N.T.*) defines "*moicheuo* in the active means 'to commit adultery' or 'to seduce', and in the passive or middle 'to be seduced'…" (p. 605)

5:28 TELL (*lego*) – In Matthew 5:28, *lego* is a first person singular present active subjunctive meaning that Jesus is telling his disciples something on an ongoing basis. Vine defines *lego* as "primarily, to pick out, gather, chiefly denotes to say, speak, affirm, whether of actual speech, e.g. Matt. 11:17, or of unspoken thought e.g., Matt. 3:9, or of a message in writing, e.g. II Cor. 8:8… A characteristic of *lego* is that it refers to the purpose or sentiment of what is said as well as the connection of the words…" (p. 323)

LOOKS (*blepo*) – In Matthew 5:28, *blepo* is a nominative singular masculine present active participle that means the act of continuous, ongoing looking at a woman to lust. Vine defines *blepo* as "to have sight, is used of bodily vision…" (p. 337)

LUSTFULLY (*epithumeo*) – In Matthew 5:28, *epithumeo* is aorist first infinitive (verbal noun) that means "to lust" at a point in time. Vine describes *epithumeo* as a "strong desire of any kind, the various kinds being frequently specified by some adjective… The word is used of good desires in Luke 22:15, Phil. 1:23; and I Thes. 2:17 only. Everywhere else it has a bad sense." (p. 25)

ALREADY (*hada*) – *Hada* is an adverb that means "before now," or "already."

COMMITTED ADULTERY (*moicheuo*) – In Matthew 5:28, *moicheuo* is a third person singular aorist first active indicative verb that means the fact of adultery having been committed at a point in time. See description of adultery above for more detailed information.

HEART (*kardia*) – Vine defines *kardia* as "man's entire mental and moral activity, both the rational and emotional elements. In other words, the heart is used figuratively for the hidden springs of the personal life." (p. 206-207) For more information see "heart" in the Matthew 5:8.

Barclay (*GOM*, Vol. 1) comments that, "according to the literal meaning of the Greek the man who is condemned is the man who looks at a woman with the deliberate intention of lusting after her. The man who is condemned is the man who deliberately uses his eyes to awaken his lust, the man who looks in such a way that passion is awakened and desire deliberately stimulated." (p. 147).

Carson (*The Sermon on the Mount*) states that, "this is not a prohibition of the normal attraction which exists between men and women, but of the deep-seated lust which consumes and devours, which on imagination attacks and rapes, which mentally contemplates and commits adultery." (p. 44)

5:29 SIN (*skandalizo*) – In Matthew 5:29, *skandalizo* is a third person singular present active indicative verb that means the ongoing fact of causing a person to stumble into sin. Vine defines *skandalizo* as "to put a snare or stumbling block in the way, always metaphorically in the N.T... (p. 130). Kittle says, "the original stem has the sense of 'springing forward and back,' 'slamming to,' 'closing on something,' or 'trapping'... " (p. 1036)

GOUGE IT OUT (*exaireo*) – In Matthew 5:29, *exaireo* is a second person singular aorist second active imperative verb that means the command to gouge out the lust at a point in time. Vine describes *exaireo* as "to take out (*ex* for *eg*, sin, in Matt. 5:29; 18:9, indicating that, with determination and promptitude, we are to strike at the root of unholy inclinations, riding ourselves of whatever would stimulate them." (p. 190)

CAST IT AWAY (*ballo*) – In Matthew 5:29, *ballo* is a second person singular aorist second active imperative verb that means the command to cast the lust away at a point in time. Vine defines *ballo* as "to throw, hurl, in contrast to striking..." (p. 171) *Ballo* is also used in Matthew 5:13 for salt that has lost its saltiness and is worthless except to be "thrown out" and trampled on.

BETTER (*sumphero*) – In Matthew 5:29, *sumphero* is third person singular present indicative verb that means the ongoing fact of it being better to cast away lust than to suffer the death of sin and hell. Vine defines *sumphero* as "(a) transitively, lit., to bring together... (b) intransitively, to be an advantage, profitable, expedient (not merely 'convenient')..." (p. 62)

LOSE (*apollumi*) – In Matthew 5:29, *apollumi* is a third person singular aorist second middle subjunctive that means that it is better for a person to lose the momentary pleasure of lust at a point in time than to suffer total condemnation as an unrepentant sinner. Vine defines *apollumi* as "to destroy, signifies, in the Middle Voice, to perish..." (p. 176)

THROWN INTO (*ballo*) – In Matthew 5:29, *ballo* is a third person singular aorist first passive subjunctive that means that a person is thrown into hell at a point in time. See description of *ballo* above for more information.

HELL (*geenna*) – See Matthew 5:22 for definition of *geenna*.

5:30 This verse is a parallel of verse 29. It uses the same verbs and tenses except for "cut it out" instead of "pluck it out."

CUT IT OUT (*ekkopto*) – In Matthew 5:30, *ekkopto* is a second person singular aorist first active imperative verb that means the command to cut the lust out of our lives at a point in time. Vine defines *ekkopto* as "to cut or strike out (*ek*, out or off, and *kopto*, to cut by a blow), to cut down…" (p. 264)

Stott (*SOM*) comments that, "what we do have liberty to say is only this (for this is what Jesus said): if your eye causes you to sin, don't look; if your foot cause you to sin, don't go; if your hand causes you to sin, don't do it… what is necessary for all those with strong sexual temptations, and indeed for all of us in principle, is discipline in guarding the approaches of sin… we shall have to eliminate from our lives certain things which (though some may be innocent in themselves) either are, or could easily become, sources of temptation." (p. 90-91)

Application (A):

What insights about discipleship have you gained from this chapter?

While praying through this list of insights, ask God which of these you are already applying and which you need to start applying. Try to identify strengths and weaknesses, and prioritize which weaknesses God wants you to work on.

Identify the top priority issue that God wants you to work on and formulate a study/application plan to allow God to graciously begin his transforming work in your heart. What is God's top priority issue and how are you going to cooperate with him in this?

Is there a mentor or accountability partner who can help you by giving wise counsel, praying, encouraging, holding you accountable, etc.? Who is it and how/when will you contact him/her?

CHAPTER 8

Matthew 5:31-32 – Divorce

⁵:³¹ It hath been said, Whosoever shall put away his wife, let him give her a writing of divorcement: ³² But I say unto you, That whosoever shall put away his wife, saving for the cause of fornication, causeth her to commit adultery: and whosoever shall marry her that is divorced committeth adultery. (KJV)

Introduction (I): Go to biblegateway.com for additional translations and paraphrases.

(NIV) ⁵:³¹ "It has been said, 'Anyone who divorces his wife must give her a certificate of divorce.' ³² But I tell you that anyone who divorces his wife, except for sexual immorality, makes her the victim of adultery, and anyone who marries a divorced woman commits adultery.

(NASB) ⁵:³¹ "It was said, 'WHOEVER SENDS HIS WIFE AWAY, LET HIM GIVE HER A CERTIFICATE OF DIVORCE'; ³² but I say to you that everyone who divorces his wife, except for the reason of unchastity, makes her commit adultery; and whoever marries a divorced woman commits adultery.

(Message) ⁵:³¹⁻³² "Remember the Scripture that says, 'Whoever divorces his wife, let him do it legally, giving her divorce papers and her legal rights'? Too many of you are using that as a cover for selfishness and whim, pretending to be righteous just because you are 'legal.' Please, no more pretending. If you divorce your wife, you're responsible for making her an adulteress (unless she has already made herself that by sexual promiscuity). And if you marry such a divorced adulteress, you're automatically an adulterer yourself. You can't use legal cover to mask a moral failure.

Discovery (D): Study Guide For Matthew 5:31-32 – Divorce

Read the passage in the KJV and respond to the following questions (note that this is the third of six consecutive Study Guide passages that include the phrases, "Ye have heard that… But I say unto you…"):

1. (5:31) What does "put away his wife [divorce]" mean? (Look up at least three other passages that use this word or phrase)

2. (5:32) What are the acceptable conditions for divorce? How does this relate to the Beatitudes and Salt and Light passages (Matthew 5:3-16)?

3. (5:31-32) Read Matthew 19:1-12 and Luke 6:18. What is Jesus telling his disciples about divorce?

4. (5:31-32) Read I Timothy 3:1-7. What are the characteristics of Christian leadership? What is the importance of healthy marriages and relationships to effectiveness as a Christian leader?

5. (5:31-32) What is your interpretation and application of this passage?

Explanation (E):

5:31 **DIVORCE** (*apoluo*) – In Matthew 5:31, *apoluo* is a third person singular first aorist active subjunctive that means an act of divorce at a point in time. Vine (*Expository Dictionary of N.T. Words*) defines *apoluo* as "to let loose, let go, free (*apo*, from, *luo*, to loose), is translated 'is divorced' in the A.V. of Matt. 5:32 (R.V., 'is put away'); it is further used of divorce in Matt. 1:19; 19:3, 7-9; Mark 10:2, 4, 11; Luke 16:18. The Lord also uses it of the case of a wife putting away her husband, Mark 10:12, a usage among Greeks and Romans, not among Jews." (p. 329)

WIFE (*gunaikeios*) – Vine comments that the root *gune* means "a woman, married or unmarried..." (p. 215) Kittle (*Theological Dictionary of the N.T.*) comments that *gune* means either "female" or "wife" depending on the context. (p. 132)

CERTIFICATE OF DIVORCE (*apostasion*) – Vine defines *apostasion* as "primarily, a defection, literally, a standing off (*apo*, from, *stasis*, a standing; cp. *Aphistemi*, to cause to withdraw), denotes in the N.T., a writing or bill of divorcement, Matt. 5:31; 19:7, Mark 10:4." (p. 329) O.T. references include Deut. 24:104, Numbers 5:12-15, Ex. 20:14.

5:32 **DIVORCE** (*apoluo*) – In Matthew 5:32, *apoluo* is nominative (verbal noun) singular present active participle that means the present action of divorce by the subject. For further information about the meaning of *apoluo*, see definition in verse 31 above.

UNFAITHFULNESS (*porneia*) – In Matthew 5:32, *porneia* is a genitive singular that is the case of possession. Vine defines *porneia* as "(a) of illicit sexual intercourse... in Matt. 5:32 and 19:9 it stands for, or includes, adultery... (b) metaphorically, of the association of pagan idolatry with doctrines of, and professed adherence to, the Christian faith..." (p. 125)

CAUSES (*poieo*) – In Matthew 5:32, *poieo* is a third person singular present active indicative verb that means the fact of causing another to commit adultery.

COMMIT ADULTERY (*moicheuo*) – In Matthew 5:32, *moicheuo* is a first aorist passive indicative (verbal noun) that means that the subject was caused to commit adultery at a point in time. Vine defines *moicheuo* as "adultery."

MARRIES (*gameo*) – In Matthew 5:32, *gameo* is a third person singular first aorist active subjunctive verb that means the act of marriage at a point in time without reference to past, present, or future.

COMMIT ADULTERY (*moicheuo*) – In Matthew 5:32, *moicheuo* is a third person singular present indicative verb that means the fact of committing adultery on an ongoing basis.

Barclay, (*GOM*, Vol. 1) comments that, "when Jesus laid down this law for marriage, he laid it down against a very definite situation. There is no time in history when the marriage bond stood in greater peril of destruction than the days when Christianity first came into this world. At that time, the world was in danger of witnessing the almost total breakup of marriage and the collapse of the home. (p. 150) Barclay further comments on the Jewish ideal and reality of marriage, "Ideally the Jew abhorred divorce. The voice of God has said, 'I hate divorce' (Malachi 2:16)… The tragedy was that practice fell so far short of the ideal. One thing vitiated the whole marriage relationship. The woman in the eyes of the law was a thing. She was at the absolute disposal of her father or her husband. She had virtually no legal rights at all. To all intents and purposes, a woman could not divorce her husband for any reason, and a man could divorce his wife for any cause at all…" (p. 151)

Stott (*SOM*) comments that there were two views of divorce in the Jewish religious culture at the time of Christ. Both of these schools of thought based their arguments on the phrase "some indecency" in Deut. 24:1. "Rabbi Shammai took a rigorous line, and taught from Deuteronomy 24:1 that the sole ground for divorce was some grave matrimonial offense, something evidently 'unseemly' or 'indecent.' Rabbi Hillel, on the other hand, held a very lax view… Similarly Hillel, arguing that the ground for divorce was something ''unseemly' interpreted this term in the widest possible way to include a wife's most trivial offenses." (p. 93) Stott further points out that the Pharisees seemed to have been attracted by Hillel's interpretation of laxity.

Stott (*SOM*) concludes that, "the only situation in which divorce and re-marriage are possible without breaking the seventh commandment is when it has already been broken by some serious sexual sin. In this case, and in this case only, Jesus seems to have taught that divorce was permissible, or at least that it could be obtained without the innocent party contracting the further stigma of adultery." (p. 97-98) Stott further comments that "for this reluctant permission of Jesus must still be seen for what it is, namely a continued accommodation to the hardness of human hearts. In addition, it must always be read both in its immediate context (Christ's emphatic endorsement of the permanence of marriage in God's purpose) and also in the wider context of the Sermon on the Mount and of the whole Bible that proclaims a gospel of reconciliation, so one must never begin a discussion on this subject by inquiring about the legitimacy of divorce. To be preoccupied with the grounds for divorce is to be guilty of the very Pharisaism which Jesus condemned. His whole emphasis in debating with the rabbis was positive, namely on God's original institution of marriage as an exclusive and permanent relationship, on God's 'yoking' of two people into a union which man must not break, and (one might add) on his call to his followers to love and forgive one another, and to be peacemakers in every situation and discord." (p. 98)

Application (A):

What insights about discipleship have you gained from this chapter?

While praying through this list of insights, ask God which of these you are already applying and which you need to start applying. Try to identify strengths and weaknesses, and prioritize which weaknesses God wants you to work on.

Identify the top priority issue that God wants you to work on and formulate a study/application plan to allow God to graciously begin his transforming work in your heart. What is God's top priority issue and how are you going to cooperate with him in this?

Is there a mentor or accountability partner who can help you by giving wise counsel, praying, encouraging, holding you accountable, etc.? Who is it and how/when will you contact him/her?

CHAPTER 9

Matthew 5:33-37 – Oaths

5:33 Again, ye have heard that it hath been said by them of old time, Thou shalt not forswear thyself, but shalt perform unto the Lord thine oaths: 34 But I say unto you, Swear not at all; neither by heaven; for it is God's throne: 35 Nor by the earth; for it is his footstool: neither by Jerusalem; for it is the city of the great King. 36 Neither shalt thou swear by thy head, because thou canst not make one hair white or black. 37 But let your communication be, Yea, yea; Nay, nay: for whatsoever is more than these cometh of evil. (KJV)

Introduction (I): Go to biblegateway.com for additional translations and paraphrases.

(NIV) 5:33 "Again, you have heard that it was said to the people long ago, 'Do not break your oath, but fulfill to the Lord the vows you have made.' 34 But I tell you, do not swear an oath at all: either by heaven, for it is God's throne; 35 or by the earth, for it is his footstool; or by Jerusalem, for it is the city of the Great King. 36 And do not swear by your head, for you cannot make even one hair white or black. 37 All you need to say is simply 'Yes' or 'No'; anything beyond this comes from the evil one.

(NASB) 5:33 "Again, you have heard that the ancients were told, 'YOU SHALL NOT MAKE FALSE VOWS, BUT SHALL FULFILL YOUR VOWS TO THE LORD.' 34 But I say to you, make no oath at all, either by heaven, for it is the throne of God, 35 or by the earth, for it is the footstool of His feet, or by Jerusalem, for it is THE CITY OF THE GREAT KING. 36 Nor shall you make an oath by your head, for you cannot make one hair white or black. 37 But let your statement be, 'Yes, yes' or 'No, no'; anything beyond these is of evil.

(Message) 5:33-37 "And don't say anything you don't mean. This counsel is embedded deep in our traditions. You only make things worse when you lay down a smoke screen of pious talk, saying, 'I'll pray for you,' and never doing it, or saying, 'God be with you,' and not meaning it. You don't make your words true by embellishing them with religious lace. In making your speech sound more religious, it becomes less true. Just say 'yes' and 'no.' When you manipulate words to get your own way, you go wrong.

Discovery (D): Study Guide For Matthew 5:33-37 – Oaths

Read the passage in the KJV and respond to the following questions (note that this is the fourth of six consecutive Study Guide passages that include the phrases, "Ye have heard that… But I say unto you…"):

1. (5:33) What does "Thou shalt not forswear thyself [promise or oath]" mean? (Look up at least three other passages that use this word or phrase)

2. (5:34) What does "Swear not at all" mean? How does this relate to the Beatitudes and Salt and Light passages (Matthew 5:3-16)?

3. (5:34-36) Why does Jesus forbid oaths with conditions like swearing "by heaven" or "by the earth" or "by thy head"?

4. (5:37) What does "Yea, yea; Nay, nay" mean? Why is adding "whatsoever" lead to "evil"?

5. (5:33-37) What is your interpretation and application of this passage?

Explanation (E):

5:33 **BREAK** (*epiorkeo*) – In Matthew 5:33, *epiorkeo* is a second person singular future indicative verb that means the fact of violating one's word in the future. Vine (*Expository Dictionary of N.T. Words*) defines *epiorkeo* as "to swear falsely, to undo one's swearing, forswear oneself (*epi*, against, *orkos*, an oath), Matt. 5:33," (p. 126) Kittle (*Theological Dictionary of the N.T.*) defines *epiorkeo* as "to be a perjurer… to break a vow." (p. 730)

OATH (*horkos*) – Vine defines *horkos* as "primarily equivalent to *herkos*, a fence, an enclosure, that which restrains a person; hence, an oath. The Lord's command in Matt. 5:33 was a condemnation of the minute and arbitrary restrictions imposed by the scribes and Pharisees in the matter of adjurations, by which God's name was profaned." (p. 123)

KEEP (*apodidomi*) – In Matthew 5:33, *apodidomi* is a second person singular future indicative verb that means the future fact of keeping one's word. Vine defines *apodidomi* as "to give back, or in full, is translated 'thou… shalt perform' in Matt. 5:33." (p. 176) Vine further notes that *apodidomi* means "to give back or up… in the sense of giving back, of the Lord's act in giving a healed boy back to this father, Luke 9:42." (p. 289)

5:34 **SWEAR** (*omnuo*) – In Matthew 5:34, *omnuo* is a first aorist infinitive (verbal noun) that means the making of an oath at a point in time. Kittle defines *omnuo* as "to swear, to affirm by oath… in the law the oath is an essential element in spite of the tendency to use it in daily life. The law prohibits false oaths and insists that oaths and vows be kept. Jesus, however, set up a new order of life in the kingdom which leaves no place for oaths since there is no reason here to suspect human veracity. Those who belong to the kingdom must always be truthful, and hence do not need to swear." (p. 683)

Barclay (*GOM*, Vol. 1) writes, "but in the time of Jesus, there were two unsatisfactory things about taking oaths. The first was what might be called frivolous swearing, taking an oath where no oath was necessary or proper. It had become far too common a custom to introduce a statement by saying, 'By thy life,' or 'By my head,' or 'May I never see the comfort of Israel if...' The Rabbis laid it down that to use any form of oath in a simple statement like: 'that is an olive tree,' was sinful and wrong. 'The yes of the righteous is yes,' they said, 'and their no is no.'... The second Jewish custom was in some ways even worse than that; it might be called evasive swearing. The Jews divided oaths into classes, those which were absolutely binding and those which were not. Any oath which contained the name of God was absolutely binding; any oath which succeeded in evading the name of god was held not to be binding. The result was that if a man swore by the name of God in any form, he would rigidly keep that oath; but if he swore by heaven or by earth, or by Jerusalem, or by his head, he felt quite free to break that oath... The idea behind this was that, if god's name was used, God became a partner in the transaction; whereas if God's name was not used, God had nothing to do with the transaction." (p. 159)

5:35 **YES** (*nai*) – Vine defines *nai* as "a particle of affirmation, is used (a) in answer to a question... (b) in assent to an assertion... (c) in confirmation of an assertion... (d) in solemn asseveration... (e) in repetition for emphasis... (f) singly in contrast to *on*, 'nay.'" (p. 243-244)

NO (*on*) – Vine defines *on* as "no, not, expressing a negative absolutely..." (p. 103)

EVIL ONE (*poneros*) – Vine says that *poneros* is used to describe "(a) of Satan as the evil one, Matt. 5:37... (b) of human beings, Matt. 5:45... (c) neuter, 'evil (things)', Matt. 9:4..." (p. 51)

Barclay (*GOM*, Vol. 1) comments that, "in effect, Jesus is saying that, so far from having to make God a partner in any transaction, no man can keep God out of any transaction. God is already there... here is a great eternal truth. Life cannot be divided into compartments in some of which God is involved and in others of which he is not involved; there cannot be one kind of language in the church and another kind of language in the shipyard or the factory or the office; there cannot be one kind of standard of conduct in the church and another kind of standard in the business world... we will regard all promises as sacred, if we remember that all promises are made in the presence of God." (p. 159-160)

Bonhoeffer (*Cost of Discipleship*) reminds us that, "there is no truth toward Jesus without truth toward man. Untruthfulness destroys fellowship, but truth cuts false fellowship to pieces and establishes genuine brotherhood. We cannot follow Christ unless we live in revealed truth before God and man." (p. 155)

Jones (*The Christ of the Mount*) comments that, "He knew that oaths were of no use — a good man would not need one, and a bad man would not heed one." (p. 159)

Stott (*SOM*) says that, "what Jesus emphasized in his teaching was that honest men do not need to resort to oaths; it was not that they should refuse to take an oath if required by some external authority to do so." (p. 102)

Application (A):

What insights about discipleship have you gained from this chapter?

While praying through this list of insights, ask God which of these you are already applying and which you need to start applying. Try to identify strengths and weaknesses, and prioritize which weaknesses God wants you to work on.

Identify the top priority issue that God wants you to work on and formulate a study/application plan to allow God to graciously begin his transforming work in your heart. What is God's top priority issue and how are you going to cooperate with him in this?

Is there a mentor or accountability partner who can help you by giving wise counsel, praying, encouraging, holding you accountable, etc.? Who is it and how/when will you contact him/her?

CHAPTER 10

Matthew 5:38-42 – Revenge

^{5:38} Ye have heard that it hath been said, An eye for an eye, and a tooth for a tooth: ³⁹ But I say unto you, That ye resist not evil: but whosoever shall smite thee on thy right cheek, turn to him the other also. ⁴⁰ And if any man will sue thee at the law, and take away thy coat, let him have thy cloak also. ⁴¹ And whosoever shall compel thee to go a mile, go with him twain. ⁴² Give to him that asketh thee, and from him that would borrow of thee turn not thou away. (KJV)

Introduction (I): Go to biblegateway.com for additional translations and paraphrases.

(NIV) ^{5:38} "You have heard that it was said, 'Eye for eye, and tooth for tooth.' ³⁹ But I tell you, do not resist an evil person. If anyone slaps you on the right cheek, turn to them the other cheek also. ⁴⁰ And if anyone wants to sue you and take your shirt, hand over your coat as well. ⁴¹ If anyone forces you to go one mile, go with them two miles. ⁴² Give to the one who asks you, and do not turn away from the one who wants to borrow from you.

(NASB) ^{5:38} "You have heard that it was said, 'AN EYE FOR AN EYE, AND A TOOTH FOR A TOOTH.' ³⁹ But I say to you, do not resist an evil person; but whoever slaps you on your right cheek, turn the other to him also. ⁴⁰ If anyone wants to sue you and take your shirt, let him have your coat also. ⁴¹ Whoever forces you to go one mile, go with him two. ⁴² Give to him who asks of you, and do not turn away from him who wants to borrow from you.

(Message) ^{5:38-42} "Here's another old saying that deserves a second look: 'Eye for eye, tooth for tooth.' Is that going to get us anywhere? Here's what I propose: 'Don't hit back at all.' If someone strikes you, stand there and take it. If someone drags you into court and sues for the shirt off your back, giftwrap your best coat and make a present of it. And if someone takes unfair advantage of you, use the occasion to practice the servant life. No more tit-for-tat stuff. Live generously.

Discovery (D): **Study Guide For Matthew 5:38-42 – Revenge**

Read the passage in the KJV and respond to the following questions (note that this is the fifth of six consecutive Study Guide passages that include the phrases, "Ye have heard that… But I say unto you…"):

1.   (5:38) What does "An eye for eye, and a tooth for a tooth" mean? (Look up at least three other passages that use this word or phrase)

2.   (5:39) What does "resist not evil" mean? How does this relate to the Beatitudes and Salt and Light passages (Matthew 5:3-16)?

3.   (5:39-41) What does "turn to him the other" and "let him have your cloak also" and "go with him twain [two miles]" mean? How is this possible?

4.   (5:42) What is Jesus' primary teaching about revenge?

5. (5:38-42) What is your interpretation and application of this passage?

Explanation (E):

5:38 **EYE FOR EYE** - Barclay (*GOM*, Vol. 1) comments that, "Jesus begins by citing the oldest law in the world—an eye for an eye, and a tooth for a tooth. The law is known as the LEXTALIONIS, and it may be described as the law of tit for tat. It appears in the earliest known code of law, the Code of Hammurabi... The principle is clear and apparently simple—if a man has inflicted an injury on any person, an equivalent injury shall be inflicted upon him. That law became part and parcel of the ethic of the Old Testament. In the Old Testament, we find it laid down no fewer than three times... (Exodus 21:23-25)... (Leviticus 24:19-20)... (Deuteronomy 19:21)." (p. 163)

5:39 **RESIST** (*anthistemi*) – In Matthew 5:39, *anthistemi* is second aorist infinitive (verbal noun) that means the act of resisting or opposing at a point in time. Vine (*Expository Dictionary of N.T. Words*) defines *anthistemi* as "to set against (*anti*, against, *histemi*, to cause to stand), used in the Middle (or Passive) Voice and in the intransitive second aorist and perfect active, signifying to withstand, oppose, resist, is translated 'to resist' in Matt. 5:39... (p. 286)

EVIL PERSON (*poneros*) – Vine defines *poneros* as "akin to *pornos*, labor, toil, denotes evil that causes labor, pain, sorrow, malignant evil..." (p. 50)

STRIKES YOU (*rhapizo*) – In Matthew 5:39, *rhapizo* is a second person singular future active indicative verb that means the future act of being hit in the face. Vine defines *rhapizo* as "primarily to strike with a rod (*rhapis*, rod), then, to strike the face with the palm of the hand or a clenched fist..." (p. 42)

TURN (*strepho*) – In Matthew 5:39, *strepho* is a second person singular first aorist active imperative verb that means the command to turn the other cheek. Vine defines *strepho* as "(1) in the Active Voice, (a) to turn (something), Matt. 5:39..." (p. 161)

Barclay (*GOM*, Vol. 1) comments that, "what Jesus is saying is this: 'Even if a man should direct at you the most deadly and calculated insult, you must on no account retaliate, and you must on no account resent it.' It will not happen very often, if at all, that anyone will slap us on the face, but time and time again life brings to us insults either great or small; and Jesus is here saying that the true Christian has learned to resent no insult and to seek retaliation for no slight." (p. 166)

5:40 **SUE YOU** (*krino*) – In Matthew 5:40, *krino* is a first aorist passive infinitive (verbal noun) that means being sued by somebody at a point in time. Vine defines *krino* as "to esteem, judge, etc. signifies to go to law…" (p. 316)

LET HIM (*aphiemi*) – In Matthew 5:40, *aphiemi* is a second person singular second aorist imperative verb that means the command to allow the one suing you for your tunic to have your cloak as well at a point in time. Vine defines *aphiemi* as "frequently denotes to let, suffer, permit…" (p. 331)

Barclay (*GOM*, Vol. 1) comments that, "the tunic, Chilton, was the long, sack-lined inner garment made of cotton or linen. The poorest man would have a change of tunics. The cloak was the great, blanket-like outer garment which a man wore as robe by day, and used as a blanket at night. Of such garments the Jew would have only one. Now it was actually the Jewish law that a man's tunic might be taken as a pledge, but not his cloak. The point is that by right a man's cloak could not be taken permanently from him. The Christian thinks not of his rights, but of his duties; not of his privileges, but of his responsibilities. The Christian is a man who has forgotten that he has any rights at all…" (p. 167)

5:41 **FORCES YOU** (*angareuo*) – In Matthew 5:41, *angareuo* is a third person singular future verb that means the future possibility of being forced to do something. Vine defines *angareuo* as "to dispatch as an *angaros* (a Persian courier kept at regular stages with power of impressing men into service), and hence, in general, to impress into service…" (p. 219)

GO WITH HIM (*hupago*) – In Matthew 5:41, *hupago* is a second person singular present imperative that means the command to go not only the expected mile but another mile as well. Vine defines *hupago* as "to go away or to go slowly away, to depart, withdraw oneself, often with the idea of going without noise or notice…" (p. 156)

Barclay (*GOM*, Vol. 1) comments that, "in an occupied country citizens could be compelled to supply food, to provide billets, to carry baggage. Sometimes the occupying power exercised this right of compulsion in the most tyrannical and unsympathetic way. Always this threat of compulsion hung over the citizens. Palestine was an occupied country. At any moment, a Jew might feel the touch of the flat of a Roman spear on his shoulder, and know that he was compelled to serve the Romans, it might be in the most menial way… What Jesus is saying is: 'Don't be always thinking of your liberty to do as you like; be always thinking of your duty and your privilege to be of service to others. When a task is laid on you, even if the task is unreasonable and hateful, don't do it as a grim duty to be resented; do it as a service to be gladly rendered.'" (p. 168-169)

5:42 **GIVE** (*didomi*) – In Matthew 5:42, *didomi* is a second person singular second aorist active imperative verb that means the command to give at a point in time to the person who asks. Vine defines *didomi* as "to give… deliver, grant, make, minister, offer, put, set, show, suffer, take, utter, yield." (p. 148)

DO NOT TURN AWAY (*apostrepho*) – In Matthew 5:42, *apostrepho* is a second person singular second aorist passive verb that means to not turn away from someone who needs to borrow something at a point in time. Vine defines *apostrepho* as "in the Passive Voice, used reflexively, to turn oneself away from Matt. 5:42…" (p. 162)

Barclay (*GOM*, Vol. 1) comments that, "finally, it is Jesus' demand that we should give to all who ask and never turn away from him who wishes to borrow. It was based on Deuteronomy 15:7-11… The point about the seventh year is that in every seventh year there was a cancellation of debts; and the grudging and calculating man might refuse to lend anything when the seventh year was near, lest the debt be cancelled and he loose what he had given… Giving was at once a privilege and an obligation for in reality all giving is nothing less than giving to God. To give to some needy person was not something which a man might choose to do; it was something he must do; if he refused, the refusal was to God." (p. 169-171)

Application (A):

What insights about discipleship have you gained from this chapter?

While praying through this list of insights, ask God which of these you are already applying and which you need to start applying. Try to identify strengths and weaknesses, and prioritize which weaknesses God wants you to work on.

Identify the top priority issue that God wants you to work on and formulate a study/application plan to allow God to graciously begin his transforming work in your heart. What is God's top priority issue and how are you going to cooperate with him in this?

Is there a mentor or accountability partner who can help you by giving wise counsel, praying, encouraging, holding you accountable, etc.? Who is it and how/when will you contact him/her?

CHAPTER 11

Matthew 5:43-48 – Enemies

5:43 Ye have heard that it hath been said, Thou shalt love thy neighbour, and hate thine enemy. 44 But I say unto you, Love your enemies, bless them that curse you, do good to them that hate you, and pray for them which despitefully use you, and persecute you; 45 That ye may be the children of your Father which is in heaven: for he maketh his sun to rise on the evil and on the good, and sendeth rain on the just and on the unjust. 46 For if ye love them which love you, what reward have ye? do not even the publicans the same? 47 And if ye salute your brethren only, what do ye more than others? do not even the publicans so? 48 Be ye therefore perfect, even as your Father which is in heaven is perfect. (KJV)

Introduction (I): Go to biblegateway.com for additional translations and paraphrases.

(NIV) 5:43 "You have heard that it was said, 'Love your neighbor and hate your enemy.' 44 But I tell you, love your enemies and pray for those who persecute you, 45 that you may be children of your Father in heaven. He causes his sun to rise on the evil and the good, and sends rain on the righteous and the unrighteous. 46 If you love those who love you, what reward will you get? Are not even the tax collectors doing that? 47 And if you greet only your own people, what are you doing more than others? Do not even pagans do that? 48 Be perfect, therefore, as your heavenly Father is perfect.

(NASB) 5:43 "You have heard that it was said, 'YOU SHALL LOVE YOUR NEIGHBOR and hate your enemy.' 44 But I say to you, love your enemies and pray for those who persecute you, 45 so that you may be sons of your Father who is in heaven; for He causes His sun to rise on the evil and the good, and sends rain on the righteous and the unrighteous. 46 For if you love those who love you, what reward do you have? Do not even the tax collectors do the same? [47] If you greet only your brothers, what more are you doing than others? Do not even the Gentiles do the same? [48] Therefore you are to be perfect, as your heavenly Father is perfect.

(Message) [5:43-47] "You're familiar with the old written law, 'Love your friend,' and its unwritten companion, 'Hate your enemy.' I'm challenging that. I'm telling you to love your enemies. Let them bring out the best in you, not the worst. When someone gives you a hard time, respond with the energies of prayer, for then you are working out of your true selves, your God-created selves. This is what God does. He gives his best—the sun to warm and the rain to nourish—to everyone, regardless: the good and bad, the nice and nasty. If all you do is love the lovable, do you expect a bonus? Anybody can do that. If you simply say hello to those who greet you, do you expect a medal? Any run-of-the-mill sinner does that. [48] "In a word, what I'm saying is, Grow up. You're kingdom subjects. Now live like it. Live out your God-created identity. Live generously and graciously toward others, the way God lives toward you."

Discovery (D): Study Guide For Matthew 5:43-48 – Enemies

Read the passage in the KJV and respond to the following questions (note that this is the last of six consecutive Study Guide passages that include the phrases, "Ye have heard that… But I say unto you…"):

1. (5:43) What does "Love thy neighbor, and hate thine enemy" mean? (Look up at least three other passages that use this word or phrase)

2. (5:44) What does "Love your enemies" mean? (Look up at least three other passages that use this word or phrase)

3. (5:44) Note that this verse gives three ways we are to love our enemies. What does each of these mean?

    - Bless them –

    - Do good to them –

    - Pray for them –

4. (5:45) Why is loving our enemies important? How does this relate to the Beatitudes and Salt and Light passages (Matthew 5:3-16)?

5. (5:46-47) What does "what reward have ye" mean now and in eternity? (Look up at least three other passages that use this word or phrase)

6. (5:48) What does "Be ye therefore perfect" mean? (Look up at least three other passages that use this word or phrase) How is this possible?

7. (5:43-48) What is your interpretation and application of this passage?

Explanation (E):

5:43 **LOVE** (*agapao*) – In Matthew 5:43, *agapao* is a second person singular future verb that means the future act of love for one's neighbor. Vine (*Expository Dictionary of N.T. Words*) defines *agapao* as "used in the New Testament (a) to describe the attitude of God toward his son, John 17:26; the human race, generally, John 3:16; Rom. 5:8; and to such as believe on the Lord Jesus Christ, particularly, John 14:21; (b) to convey his will to his children concerning their attitude one toward another, John 13:34, and toward all men, I Thes. 3:12; I Cor. 16:14; 2 Pet 1:7; (c) to express the essential nature of God, I John 4:8. Love can be known only from the action it prompts." (p. 20-21) For a full description of the qualities of *agapao* love see I Cor. 13.

NEIGHBOR (*plesion*) – Vine defines *plesion* as "the (one) near; hence one's neighbor..." (p. 107)

HATE (*miseo*) – In Matthew 5:43, *miseo* is a second person singular future active indicative verb that means the future fact of hating one's enemy. Vine defines *miseo* as "especially (a) of malicious and unjustifiable feelings towards others... (b) of a right feeling of aversion from what is evil... (c) of relative preference for one thing over another... " (p. 198)

ENEMY (*echithros*) – Vine defines *echithros* as "primarily denoting hating or hateful (akin to *echthos*, hate; perhaps associated with *ektos*, outside), hence, in the active sense, denotes hating; hostile; it is used as a noun signifying an enemy, adversary..." (p. 30)

5:44 **LOVE** (*agapao*) – In Matthew 5:44, *agapao* is a second person plural present imperative verb that means the command to love on an ongoing basis. See description of *agapao* in verse 43.

ENEMY (*echithros*) – see description in verse 43 for definition of *echithros*.

PRAY (*prosenchomai*) – in Matthew 5:44, *prosenchomai* is a second person plural present imperative verb that means the command to pray for those who persecute you on an ongoing basis. Vine defines *prosenchomai* as "to pray, is always used of prayer to God, and is the most frequent word in this respect..." (p. 199)

PERSECUTE (*dioko*) – In Matthew 5:44, *dioko* is a genitive plural masculine present active participle that means the ongoing action of persecution. Vine defines *dioko* as "(a) to put to flight, drive away, (b) to pursue, whence the meaning to persecute, Matt. 5:10-12, 44..." (p. 177-178)

5:45 **SONS OF YOUR FATHER IN HEAVEN** (*huios*) – See Matthew 5:9 ("Peacemakers") for description of *huios*.

CAUSES (*anatello*) – In Matthew 5:45, *anatello* is third person singular present indicative that means the fact of God causing the sun to rise on the evil and the just on an ongoing basis. Vine defines *anatello* as "to arise, is used especially of things in the natural creation..." (p. 74)

EVIL (*poneros*) - See Matthew 5:39 ("Revenge") for definition of *poneros*.

GOOD (*agathos*) – Vine defines *agathos* as "that which, being good in its character or constitution, is beneficial in it effects..." (p. 163)

RIGHTEOUS (*dikaios*) – Vine defines *dikaios* as "used of a person observant of *dike*, custom, rule, right, especially in fulfillment of duties toward God and men, and of the things that were in accordance with right." (p. 283)

UNRIGHTEOUS (*adikos*) – Vine defines *adikos* as "not in conformity with *dike*, right, is rendered 'unjust' in the A.V. and R.V. in Matt. 5:45..." (p. 171)

5:46 **LOVE** (*agapao*) – In Matthew 5:46, *agapao* is a second person plural first aorist imperative verb that means the command to love the one loving you at a point in time. See definition of *agapao* in verse 43 above.

REWARD (*misthos*) – Vine defines *misthos* as "primarily wages, hire, and then, generally, reward…" (p. 294)

TAX COLLECTORS (*telones*) – Kittle (*Theological Dictionary of the N.T.*) describes *telones* as "the NT agrees with the rabbis in thinking that tax collectors alienate themselves from God and the people. 'Publicans and sinners' are the opposite of the children of the kingdom (cf. Matt. 5:46-47). Tax collectors are notoriously wicked Israelites who may even be grouped with the Gentiles (cf. Matt. 18:15 ff.). If the interest of the NT is in the conversion, as in Luke 18:9 ff. and 19:1 f., it is as an example of God's miraculous power to bring even the most sinful back to himself." (p. 1168)

5:47 **GREET** (*aspazomai*) – In Matthew 5:47, *aspazomai* is a second person plural first aorist subjuntive verb that means the act of greeting at a point in time without reference as to the time past, present, or future. Vine defines *aspazomai* as "to greet, welcome, or salute… The verb is used as a technical term for conveying greetings at the close of a letter, often by an amanuensis." (p. 177)

GENTILES (*ethnos*) – Vine defines *ethnos* as "firstly, a multitude or company; then, a multitude of people of the same nature or genus, a nation, people; it is used in the singular, of the Jews, e.g., Luke 7:5; 23:2…; in the plural of nations (Heb., *goiim*) other than Israel, e.g., Matt. 4:15; Rom. 3:29; 11:11…" (p. 144)

5:48 **PERFECT** (*teleios*) – Vine defines *teleios* as "having reached its end (*telos*), finished, compete, perfect." (p. 173-174) Kittle says of *teleios* that, "the N.T. never seems to use *teleios* for a gradual advance to Christian perfection… It plainly means 'whole' or 'entire' in Matthew, Paul, and the Catholic Epistles, and it also has the sense of 'mature' in some passages in Paul." (p. 1165)

FATHER (*pater*) – Vine defines *pater* as "a nourisher, protector, upholder…" (p. 81)

Bonhoeffer (*Cost of Discipleship*) writes that, "the will of God, to which the law gives expression, is that men should defeat their enemies by loving them… The Christian must treat his enemy as a brother, and require his hostility with love. His behavior must be determined not by the way others treat him, but by the treatment he himself receives from Jesus…" (p. 164)

Application (A):

What insights about discipleship have you gained from this chapter?

While praying through this list of insights, ask God which of these you are already applying and which you need to start applying. Try to identify strengths and weaknesses, and prioritize which weaknesses God wants you to work on.

Identify the top priority issue that God wants you to work on and formulate a study/application plan to allow God to graciously begin his transforming work in your heart. What is God's top priority issue and how are you going to cooperate with him in this?

Is there a mentor or accountability partner who can help you by giving wise counsel, praying, encouraging, holding you accountable, etc.? Who is it and how/when will you contact him/her?

CHAPTER 12

Matthew 6:1-4 – Giving

⁶:¹ Take heed that ye do not your alms before men, to be seen of them: otherwise ye have no reward of your Father which is in heaven. ² Therefore when thou doest thine alms, do not sound a trumpet before thee, as the hypocrites do in the synagogues and in the streets, that they may have glory of men. Verily I say unto you, They have their reward. ³ But when thou doest alms, let not thy left hand know what thy right hand doeth: ⁴ That thine alms may be in secret: and thy Father which seeth in secret himself shall reward thee openly. (KJV)

Introduction (I): Go to biblegateway.com for additional translations and paraphrases.

(NIV) ⁶:¹ "Be careful not to practice your righteousness in front of others to be seen by them. If you do, you will have no reward from your Father in heaven. ² "So when you give to the needy, do not announce it with trumpets, as the hypocrites do in the synagogues and on the streets, to be honored by others. Truly I tell you, they have received their reward in full. ³ But when you give to the needy, do not let your left hand know what your right hand is doing, ⁴ so that your giving may be in secret. Then your Father, who sees what is done in secret, will reward you.

(NASB) ⁶:¹ "Beware of practicing your righteousness before men to be noticed by them; otherwise you have no reward with your Father who is in heaven. ² "So when you give to the poor, do not sound a trumpet before you, as the hypocrites do in the synagogues and in the streets, so that they may be honored by men. Truly I say to you, they have their reward in full. ³ But when you give to the poor, do not let your left hand know what your right hand is doing, ⁴ so that your giving will be in secret; and your Father who sees what is done in secret will reward you.

(Message) [6:1] "Be especially careful when you are trying to be good so that you don't make a performance out of it. It might be good theater, but the God who made you won't be applauding. [2-4] "When you do something for someone else, don't call attention to yourself. You've seen them in action, I'm sure—'playactors' I call them—treating prayer meeting and street corner alike as a stage, acting compassionate as long as someone is watching, playing to the crowds. They get applause, true, but that's all they get. When you help someone out, don't think about how it looks. Just do it—quietly and unobtrusively. That is the way your God, who conceived you in love, working behind the scenes, helps you out.

Discovery (D): Study Guide For Matthew 6:1-4 – Giving

Read the passage in the KJV and respond to the following questions:

1. (6:1) What does "do not your alms [gifts] before men" mean? (Look up at least three other passages that use this word or phrase)

2. (6:1) What does "no reward of your Father" mean? (Look up at least three other passages that use this word or phrase)

3. (6:2) What does "hypocrites" mean? (Look up at least three other passages that use this word or phrase) What are the actions of hypocrites?

4. (6:3-4) What does "That thine alms be in secret" mean? Why is this important?

5. (6:4) What does "thy Father which sees in secret himself shall reward thee openly" mean? How does this relate to the Beatitudes and Salt and Light passages (Matthew 5:3-16)?

6. What is your interpretation and application of this passage?

Explanation (E):

6:1 **CAREFUL** (*prosecho*) – In Matthew 6:1, *prosecho* is a second person plural present imperative verb that means the command to "take heed" on an ongoing basis. Vine (*Expository Dictionary of N.T. Words*) defines *prosecho* as "to hold to, signifies to turn to, turn one's attention to; hence, to give heed…" (p. 211)

TO DO (*poieo*) – In Matthew 6:1, *poieo* is a present active infinitive (verbal noun) that means doing something on an ongoing basis. Vine defines *poieo* as "chiefly to make, produce, create, cause…" (p. 330)

RIGHTEOUSNESS (*dikaiosune*) – Vine defines *dikaiosune* as "the character of quality of being right or just…" (p. 298) See Matthew 5:6 ("Those Who Hunger and Thirst After Righteousness") for further description of *dikaiosune*.

TO BE SEEN (*pheaomai*) – In Matthew 6:1, *pheaomai* is a first aorist passive infinitive (verbal noun) that means being seen at a point in time. Green (*Greek and English Lexicon to the N.T.*) defines *pheaomai* as "to gaze upon... to see, discern with the eyes..." (p. 83)

HAVE NO (*echo*) – In Matthew 6:1, *echo* is a third person plural present imperative that means the command to have no reward on an ongoing basis. Vine defines *echo* as "to hold, in the hand... to hold fast, keep..." (p. 199)

REWARD (*misthos*) – Vine defines *misthos* as "primarily wages, hire, and then, generally, reward..." (p. 294) See Matthew 5:10-12 ("Those Who Are Persecuted Because of Righteousness") for further description of *misthos*.

6:2 **GIVE** (*poieo*) – In Matthew 6:2, *poieo* is a third person singular present active subjunctive verb that means the ongoing action of giving. Kittle (*Theological Dictionary of the N.T.*) defines *poieo* as "to create, make, do, act." (p. 895)

NEEDY [ALMS] (*eleemosune*) – Vine defines *eleemosune* as "connected with *eleemon*, merciful, signifies (a) mercy, pity, particularly in giving alms, Matt. 6:1-4; Acts 10:2; 24:17; (b) the benefaction itself, the alms (the effect for the cause), Luke 11:41; 12:33; Acts 3:2, 3, 10; 9:36..." (p. 48-49)

ANNOUNCE (*salpizo*) – In Matthew 6:2, *salpizo* is a second person singular first aorist subjunctive verb that means an announcement at a point in time without reference to past, present, or future. Vine defines *salpizo* as "to sound a trumpet..." (p. 55)

HYPOCRITES (*hupokrisis*) – Vine defines *hupokrisis* as "primarily denotes a reply, an answer (akin to *hupokrinomai*, to answer); then, play-acting, as the actors spoke in dialogue; hence, pretence, hypocracy..." (p. 241) Kittle writes of *hupokrinomai* that, "a pious appearance and a distinction of proportion concealed the failure to do God's will. In contrast, the disciples must achieve a greater righteousness (Matt. 5:20), showing a concern for integrity rather than status (6:2ff.)..." (p. 1236)

HONORED BY MEN (*doxazo*) – In Matthew 6:2, *doxazo* is a third person plural first aorist passive subjunctive verb that means to be honored by men at a point in time without reference to past, present, or future time. Vine defines *doxazo* as "to glorify... is rendered 'honor' and 'honorith' in the A.V. of John 8:54..." (p. 231) Kittle defines *doxazo* as "while individual nuances may embrace divine honor, splendor, power, or radiance, what is always expressed is the divine mode of being..." (p. 180)

RECEIVED [Have] (*apecho*) – In Matthew 6:2, *apecho* is a third person plural present active indicative verb that means the ongoing fact of receiving the reward. Vine defines *apecho* as "(a) transitively, to have in full, to have received… (b) intransitively, to be away, distant…" (p. 257)

REWARD (*misthos*) – see definition for *misthos* in verse 6:1 above.

6:3 **GIVE** (*poieo*) – In Matthew 6:3, *poieo* is a genative masculine singular present active participle that means the act of ongoing giving. See definition of *poieo* in verse 6:2 above.

NEEDY [ALMS] (*eleemosune*) – See definition of *eleemosune* in verse 6:2 above.

DO NOT LET KNOW (*ginosko*) – In Matthew 6:3, *ginosko* is a third person singular second aorist active imperative verb that means the command to not let your one hand know what your other hand is giving at a point in time. Vine defines *ginosko* as "to be taking in knowledge, to come to know, recognize, understand, or to understand completely…" (p.297)

6:4 **GIVING [ALMS]** (*eleemosune*) – See definition of *eleemosune* in verse 6:2 above.

SECRET (*kruptos*) – Vine defines *kruptos* as "secret, hidden (akin to *krupto*, to hide), Eng. Crypt, cryptic etc., is used as an adjective and rendered 'secret' in Luke 8:17; A.V. (R.V., 'hid'); in the neuter, with *en*, in, as an adverbial phrase, 'in secret,' with the article, Matt. 6:4, 6…" (p. 335)

FATHER (*pater*) – Vine defines *pater* as "a nourisher, protector, upholder…" (p. 81)

SEES (*blepo*) – In Matthew 6:4, *blepo* is a nominative masculine singular present active participle that means seeing our secrets on an ongoing basis. Vine defines *blepo* as "(a) bodily and (b) mental vision, (a) to perceive, e.g. Matt. 13:13; (b) to take heed, e.g. Mark 13:23, 33; it indicates greater vividness than *horao*, expressing a more intent, earnest, contemplation…" (p. 114)

SECRET (*kruptos*) – See defintion of *kruptos* in verse 6:4 above.

WILL REWARD [YOU] (*apodidomai*) – In Matthew 6:4, *apodidomai* is a third person singular future active indicative verb that means the future fact of being given a reward. Vine defines *apodidomai* as "to give up or back, restore, return, is translated 'shall recompense' in the R.V. of Matt. 6:4, 6, 18 (A.V. 'shall reward')…" (p. 260)

Stott (*SOM*) writes that, "Christian giving is to be marked by self-sacrifice and self-forgetfulness, not by self-congratulations. What we should seek when giving to the needy is neither the praise of men, nor a ground of self-commendation, but rather the approval of God." (p. 131)

Application (A):

What insights about discipleship have you gained from this chapter?

While praying through this list of insights, ask God which of these you are already applying and which you need to start applying. Try to identify strengths and weaknesses, and prioritize which weaknesses God wants you to work on.

Identify the top priority issue that God wants you to work on and formulate a study/application plan to allow God to graciously begin his transforming work in your heart. What is God's top priority issue and how are you going to cooperate with him in this?

Is there a mentor or accountability partner who can help you by giving wise counsel, praying, encouraging, holding you accountable, etc.? Who is it and how/when will you contact him/her?

CHAPTER 13

Matthew 6:5-15 – Prayer

⁶:⁵ And when thou prayest, thou shalt not be as the hypocrites are: for they love to pray standing in the synagogues and in the corners of the streets, that they may be seen of men. Verily I say unto you, They have their reward. ⁶ But thou, when thou prayest, enter into thy closet, and when thou hast shut thy door, pray to thy Father which is in secret; and thy Father which seeth in secret shall reward thee openly. ⁷ But when ye pray, use not vain repetitions, as the heathen do: for they think that they shall be heard for their much speaking. ⁸ Be not ye therefore like unto them: for your Father knoweth what things ye have need of, before ye ask him. ⁹ After this manner therefore pray ye:

Our Father which art in heaven, Hallowed be thy name.

¹⁰ Thy kingdom come, Thy will be done in earth, as it is in heaven.

¹¹ Give us this day our daily bread.

¹² And forgive us our debts, as we forgive our debtors.

¹³ And lead us not into temptation, but deliver us from evil: For thine is the kingdom, and the power, and the glory, for ever. Amen.

¹⁴ For if ye forgive men their trespasses, your heavenly Father will also forgive you: ¹⁵ But if ye forgive not men their trespasses, neither will your Father forgive your trespasses. (KJV)

Introduction (I): Go to biblegateway.com for additional translations and paraphrases.

(NIV) 6:5 "And when you pray, do not be like the hypocrites, for they love to pray standing in the synagogues and on the street corners to be seen by others. Truly I tell you, they have received their reward in full. 6 But when you pray, go into your room, close the door and pray to your Father, who is unseen. Then your Father, who sees what is done in secret, will reward you. 7 And when you pray, do not keep on babbling like pagans, for they think they will be heard because of their many words. 8 Do not be like them, for your Father knows what you need before you ask him. 9 "This, then, is how you should pray:

'Our Father in heaven, hallowed be your name,
10 your kingdom come, your will be done, on earth as it is in heaven.
11 Give us today our daily bread.
12 And forgive us our debts, as we also have forgiven our debtors.
13 And lead us not into temptation, but deliver us from the evil one.'

14 For if you forgive other people when they sin against you, your heavenly Father will also forgive you. 15 But if you do not forgive others their sins, your Father will not forgive your sins.

(NASB) 6:5 "When you pray, you are not to be like the hypocrites; for they love to stand and pray in the synagogues and on the street corners so that they may be seen by men. Truly I say to you, they have their reward in full. 6 But you, when you pray, go into your inner room, close your door and pray to your Father who is in secret, and your Father who sees what is done in secret will reward you. 7 "And when you are praying, do not use meaningless repetition as the Gentiles do, for they suppose that they will be heard for their many words. 8 So do not be like them; for your Father knows what you need before you ask Him. 9 "Pray, then, in this way:

'Our Father who is in heaven,
Hallowed be Your name.
10 'Your kingdom come.
Your will be done,
On earth as it is in heaven.
11 'Give us this day our daily bread.
12 'And forgive us our debts, as we also have forgiven our debtors.
13 'And do not lead us into temptation, but deliver us from evil. [For Yours is the kingdom and the power and the glory forever. Amen.']

¹⁴ For if you forgive others for their transgressions, your heavenly Father will also forgive you. ¹⁵ But if you do not forgive others, then your Father will not forgive your transgressions.

(Message) ⁶:⁵ "And when you come before God, don't turn that into a theatrical production either. All these people making a regular show out of their prayers, hoping for stardom! Do you think God sits in a box seat? ⁶ "Here's what I want you to do: Find a quiet, secluded place so you won't be tempted to role-play before God. Just be there as simply and honestly as you can manage. The focus will shift from you to God, and you will begin to sense his grace. ⁷⁻¹³ "The world is full of so-called prayer warriors who are prayer-ignorant. They're full of formulas and programs and advice, peddling techniques for getting what you want from God. Don't fall for that nonsense. This is your Father you are dealing with, and he knows better than you what you need. With a God like this loving you, you can pray very simply. Like this:

Our Father in heaven, Reveal who you are.
Set the world right; Do what's best— as above, so below.
Keep us alive with three square meals.
Keep us forgiven with you and forgiving others.
Keep us safe from ourselves and the Devil.
You're in charge! You can do anything you want!
You're ablaze in beauty!
Yes. Yes. Yes.

¹⁴⁻¹⁵ "In prayer there is a connection between what God does and what you do. You can't get forgiveness from God, for instance, without also forgiving others. If you refuse to do your part, you cut yourself off from God's part.

Discovery (D): Study Guide For Matthew 6:5-15 – Prayer

Read the passage in the KJV and respond to the following questions:

1. (6:5) What is wrong with the way the "hypocrites" pray? How does this relate to what Jesus has to say about giving in Matthew 6:1-4?

2. (6:6) What does the Bible have to say about prayer? (Look up at least 10 other passages that use this word or phrase – make sure to include I Timothy 2: 1-4)

3. (6:6) What does "enter into thy closet" mean as it related to prayer? How does this relate to what Jesus has to say about giving in Matthew 6:1-4?

4. (6:7-8) How do the heathen pray and how is this different from the type of prayer that God prefers?

5. (6:9-13) How are followers of Jesus suppose to pray? (Note the following sequence as a pattern for prayer)

    • Our Father… Hallowed be thy name (Praise) –

- Thy kingdom come… in earth, as it is in heaven (Proclamation) –

- Give us this day our daily bread (Petition) –

- Forgive us… as we forgive our debtors (Propitiation) –

- Lead us not into temptation… deliver us from evil (Provision) –

- For thine is the kingdom (Praise and Proclamation) –

6. (6:14-15) What does "forgive men their trespasses" mean? Why is it important for us to receive forgiveness from God? (Note that prayer for forgiveness is linked with forgiving "our debtors" in Matthew 6:12)

7. (6:5-15) What is your interpretation and application of this passage?

Explanation (E):

6:5 **WHEN YOU PRAY** (*proseuchomai*) – In Matthew 6:5, *proseuchomai* is a second person plural present subjunctive which means the ongoing act of praying. Vine (*Expository Dictionary of N.T. Words*) defines *proseuchomai* as "to pray, is always used of prayer to God, and it is the most frequent word in this respect..." (p. 199) Kittle (*Theological Dictionary of the N.T.*) defines *proseuchomai* as "'to pray,' 'to pray to,' 'to ask,' 'prayer,' 'petitioning prayer.' While *deisthai* almost always denotes asking, *prosecuchesthai* contains no narrower definition of content and refers to calling on God." (p. 284)

Barclay (*GOM*, Vol. 1) writes that, "there are two things the daily use of which was prescribed for every Jew. The first was *shema*, which consists of three short passages of Scripture— Deuteronomy 6:4-9; 11:13-21; Numbers 15:37-41. *Shema* is the imperative of the Hebrew word to hear, and the *shema* takes its name from the verse which was the essence and center of the whole matter: 'Hear, O Israel, the Lord our God is one God.' The full *shema* had to be recited by every Jew every morning and every evening... The second thing which every Jew must daily repeat was called *shemoneh esreh* which means the eighteen. It consists of eighteen prayers and was, and still is, an essential part of the Synogogue service... The law was that the Jew must recite it three times a day, once in the morning, once in the afternoon, and once in the evening." (p. 192-193)

DO NOT BE LIKE THE HYPOCRITES (*hupokrites*) – Vine defines *hupokrites* as "primarily denotes one who answers; then, a stage-actor; it was a custom for Greek and Roman actors to speak in large masks with mechanical devices for augmenting the force of the voice; hence the word became used metaphorically as a dissembler, a hypocrite." (p. 242)

SEEN BY MEN (*phaino*) – In Matthew 6:5, *phaino* is a third person plural second aorist passive subjunctive verb that means to be seen by others at a point in time without reference to past, present, or future. Vine defines *phaino* as "to cause to appear, and in the Passive Voice, to appear, to manifest, is rendered '(that) they may be seen' in Matt. 6:5..." (p. 338)

Barclay (*GOM*, Vol. 1) writes that, "the Jewish system of prayer made ostentation very easy. The Jew prayed standing, with hands stretched out, palms upwards, and with head bowed. Prayer had to be said at 9 a.m., 12 midday, and 3 pm. It had to be said wherever a man might be, and it was easy for a man to make sure that these hours he was at a busy street corner, or in a crowded city square, so that all the world might see with what devotion he prayed." (p. 197)

RECEIVED THEIR REWARD (*misthos*) – Vine defines *misthos* as "primarily wages, hire, and then, generally, reward..." (p. 294) In this verse, *misthos* is the object of the third person plural present active indicative verb *apecho* ("have," "receive") that means the fact of receiving one's reward on an ongoing basis in the present.

6:6 BUT WHEN YOU PRAY (*proseuchomai*) – In Matthew 6:6, *proseuchomai* is a second person singular present subjunctive that means the ongoing act of praying.

ENTER (*eiserchomai*) – In Matthew 6:6, *eiserchomai* is a second person singular second aorist imperative verb that means the command to enter in to the privacy of one's room at a point in time.

PRAY (*proseuchomai*) – In Matthew 6:6, *proseuchomai* is a second person first aorist imperative verb that means the command to pray at a point in time.

TO THE FATHER (*pater*) – Vine defines *pater* as "a nourisher, protector, upholder..." (p. 81)

SECRET (*kruptos*) – Vine defines *kruptos* as "secret, hidden (akin to *krupto*, to hide)..." (p. 335)

WILL REWARD (*apodidomi*) – In Matthew 6:6, *apodidomi* is a third person singular future active indicative verb that means the fact of receiving a reward in the future from God. Vine defines *apodidomi* as "to give back, restore, return..." (p. 260)

6:7 WHEN YOU PRAY (*proseuchomai*) – In Matthew 6:7, *proseuchomai* is a nominative plural masculine present participle that means the ongoing action of praying.

DO NOT UTTER EMPTY WORDS (*battalogeo*) – In Matthew 6:7, *battalogeo* is a second person plural first aorist subjunctive verb that means the utterance of repetitious prayer at a point in time without reference to the past, present, or future time. Vine defines *battalogeo* as "to repeat idly, is used in Matt. 6:7 ('use not vain repetition'); the meaning to stammer is scarcely to be associated with this word. The word is probably from an Aramaic phrase... The rendering of... is 'do not be saying *battalatha*, idle things,' i.e., meaningless and mechanically repeated phrases, the reference being to pagan (not Jewish) modes of prayer." (p. 281)

6:8 WHAT YOU NEED (*chreia*) – Vine defines *chreia* as "a necessity, what must needs be..." (p. 104)

BEFORE YOU ASK HIM (*aiteo*) – In Matthew 6:8, *aiteo* is a first aorist active infinitive (verbal noun) that means that God knows our needs fully at a point in time prior to our asking him to meet them. Vine defines *aiteo* as "frequently suggests the attitude of a supplicant, the petition of one who is a lesser in position than he to whom the petition is made..." (p. 79)

6:9 **PRAY** (*proseuchomai*) – In Matthew 6:9, *proseuchomai* is a second person plural present imperative verb that means the command to pray on an ongoing basis. Vine defines *proseuchomai* as "to pray, is always used of prayer to God, and is the most frequent word in this respect…" (p. 199)

FATHER (*pater*) – Vine defines *pater* as "a nourisher, protector, upholder…" (p. 81)

HEAVEN (*ouranos*) – Vine defines *ouranos* as "to lift, to heave… In the present life heaven is the region of the spiritual citizenship of believers, Phil. 3:20." (p. 208-209) This is the same word as used in Matthew 5:3 and 5:10 for "kingdom of heaven."

HALLOWED (*agiazo*) – In Matthew 5:9, *agiazo* is a third person singular first aorist passive imperative that means the command to hallow God's name at a point in time. Vine defines *agiazo* as "to make holy (from *hagios*, holy), signifies (a) to set apart for God, to sanctify, to make a person or thing the opposite of *koinos*, common…" (p. 190)

6:10 **KINGDOM** (*basileia*) – Vine defines *basileia* as "an abstract noun, denoting sovereignty, royal power, dominion…" (p. 294)

COME (*erchomai*) – In Matthew 6:10, *erchomai* is a third person singular first aorist imperative that means the command that God's kingdom come in its fullness at a point in time. Vine defines *erchomai* as "the most frequent verb denoting either to come, or to go, signifies the act, in contrast with *heko*… which stresses the arrival…" (p. 203)

WILL (*thelema*) – Vine defines *thelema* as "(a) objectively, that which is willed, of the will of God, e.g. Matt. 18:14; Mark 3:35, the fulfilling being a sign of spiritual relationship to the Lord… (b) subjectively, the will being spoken of as the emotion of being desirous, rather than the thing willed…" (p. 216-217)

DONE (*ginomai*) – In Matthew 6:10, *ginomai* is a third person singular first aorist passive imperative verb that means the command that God's will be done at a point in time. Vine defines *ginomai* as "to become, is sometimes translated 'do' or 'done'…" (p. 330)

ON EARTH (*ge*) – Vine defines *ge* as "(a) earth as arable land, e.g., Matt. 13:5, 8, 23; in I Cor. 15:47 it is said of the earthly material of which 'the first man' was made… (b) the earth as a whole, the world, in contrast, whether of the heavens, e.g. Matt 5:18, 35 or to Heaven, the abode of God, e.g., Matt. 6:19…" (p. 12-13)

IN HEAVEN (*ouranos*) – Same word as used in Matthew 6:9 for "our father in heaven."

6:11 **GIVE US** (*didomi*) – In Matthew 6:11, *didomi* is a second person singular second aorist active imperative verb that means the command for God to give us our daily bread at a point in time. Vine defines *didomi* as "to give, is used with various meanings according to the context…" (p. 148)

DAILY BREAD (*artos*) – Vine defines *artos* as "bread (perhaps derived from *aro*, to fit together, or from a root *ar-*, the earth), signifies (a) a small loaf or cake, composed of flour and water, and baked, in shape either oblong or round, and about as thick as the thumb; these were not cut, but broken and were consecrated to the Lord every Sabbath and called the shewbread (loaves of presentation)… (b) the loaf of the Lord's supper… (c) bread of any kind… (d) metaphorically, of Christ as the Bread of God, and of Life… (e) food in general, the necessities of the sustenance of life, Matt. 6:11…" (p. 146-147)

6:12 **FORGIVE US** (*aphiemi*) – In Matthew 6:12, *aphiemi* is a second person singular second aorist imperative verb that means the command for us to ask God's forgiveness at a point in time. Vine defines *aphiemi* as "primarily, to send forth, send away (*apo*, from, *heimi*, to send), denotes, besides its other meanings; to remit or forgive (a) debts, Matt. 6:12; 18:27, 32, these being completely cancelled; (b) sins, e.g., Matt. 9:2, 5, 6… In this latter respect the verb… firstly signifies the remission of the punishment due to sinful conduct… secondly, it involves the complete removal of the cause of offense…" (p. 122)

DEBTS (*opheilema*) – Vine defines *opheilema* as "expressing debt more concretely [than *opheile*], is used (a) literally, of that which is legally due, Rom. 4:4; (b) metaphorically, of sin as a debt, because it demands expiation, and thus payment by way of punishment, Matt. 6:12." (p. 277)

HAVE FORGIVEN (*aphiemi*) – In Matthew 6:12, *aphiemi* is a first person plural first aorist active indicative verb that means the fact of having forgiven my debtors at a point in past time. The word used for forgive here is the same word as used earlier in this verse for "forgive us…"

DEBTORS (*opheiletes*) – Vine defines *opheiletes* as "one who owes anything to another, primarily in regard to money… of those who have not yet made amends to those whom they have injured, Matt. 6:12…" (p. 277-278)

6:13 **LEAD US NOT** (*eiserchomai*) – In Matthew 6:13, *eiserchomai* is a second person singular first aorist subjunctive verb that means the request to not enter into temptation at a point in time without reference for past, present, or future time. Vine defines *eiserchomai* as "to come into (*eis*, in, *erchomai*, to come), is frequently rendered 'entered' in the R.V…" (p. 34)

TEMPTATION (*peirasmos*) – Vine defines *peirasmos* as "(1) trials with a beneficial purpose and effect... (2) of trial definitely designed to lead to wrong doing.. (3) of trying or challenging God, by men... " (p. 117)

DELIVER US (*rhuomai*) – In Matthew 6:12, *rhuomai* is a second person singular first aorist imperative verb that means the command to rescue us from the evil one at a point in time. Vine defines *rhumai* as "to rescue from, preserve from, and so, to deliver..." (p. 289)

EVIL ONE (*poneros*) – Vine defines *poneros* as "of Satan as the evil one, Matt. 5:37; 6:13: 13:19, 38..." (p. 51)

SINS (*paraptoma*) – Vine defines *paraptoma* as "primarily a false step, a blunder (akin to *parapipto*, to fall away, Heb. 6:6) lit., 'a fall beside,' used ethically, denotes a trespass, a deviation, from uprightness and truth, Matt. 6:14, 15 (twice)... *paraptoma* and *hamartema* (a sinful deed) are closely associated, with regard to their primary meanings: *Parabasis* seems to be a stronger term, as a breach of a known law..." (p. 154-155)

Bonhoeffer (*The Cost of Discipleship*) states that, "Jesus told his disciples not only how to pray, but also what to pray. The Lord's Prayer is not merely the pattern prayer, it is the way Christians must pray." (p. 184)

Carson (*The Sermon on The Mount*) states that, "there are six petitions in this prayer. It is appropriate that the first three concern God directly: His name, his kingdom, his will. The Christian's primary concerns therefore are that God's name be hallowed, that his kingdom come, that his will be done on earth as it is in heaven. Only then are the next three petitions introduced, and they have to do with man directly: Our daily food, our sins ('our debts') and our temptations." (p. 61-62)

See Barclay (*GOM*, Vol. 1) and Stott (*SOM*) for excellent commentary on the "Lord's Prayer."

Application (A):

What insights about discipleship have you gained from this chapter?

While praying through this list of insights, ask God which of these you are already applying and which you need to start applying. Try to identify strengths and weaknesses, and prioritize which weaknesses God wants you to work on.

Identify the top priority issue that God wants you to work on and formulate a study/application plan to allow God to graciously begin his transforming work in your heart. What is God's top priority issue and how are you going to cooperate with him in this?

Is there a mentor or accountability partner who can help you by giving wise counsel, praying, encouraging, holding you accountable, etc.? Who is it and how/when will you contact him/her?

CHAPTER 14

Matthew 6:16-18 – Fasting

⁶:¹⁶ **Moreover when ye fast, be not, as the hypocrites, of a sad countenance: for they disfigure their faces, that they may appear unto men to fast. Verily I say unto you, They have their reward. ¹⁷ But thou, when thou fastest, anoint thine head, and wash thy face; ¹⁸ That thou appear not unto men to fast, but unto thy Father which is in secret: and thy Father, which seeth in secret, shall reward thee openly.** (KJV)

Introduction (I):   Go to biblegateway.com for additional translations and paraphrases.

(NIV)   ⁶:¹⁶ "When you fast, do not look somber as the hypocrites do, for they disfigure their faces to show others they are fasting. Truly I tell you, they have received their reward in full. ¹⁷ But when you fast, put oil on your head and wash your face, ¹⁸ so that it will not be obvious to others that you are fasting, but only to your Father, who is unseen; and your Father, who sees what is done in secret, will reward you.

(NASB)   ⁶:¹⁶ "Whenever you fast, do not put on a gloomy face as the hypocrites do, for they neglect their appearance so that they will be noticed by men when they are fasting. Truly I say to you, they have their reward in full. ¹⁷ But you, when you fast, anoint your head and wash your face ¹⁸ so that your fasting will not be noticed by men, but by your Father who is in secret; and your Father who sees what is done in secret will reward you.

(Message)   ⁶:¹⁶⁻¹⁸ "When you practice some appetite-denying discipline to better concentrate on God, don't make a production out of it. It might turn you into a small-time celebrity but it won't make you a saint. If you 'go into training' inwardly, act normal outwardly. Shampoo and comb your hair, brush your teeth, wash your face. God doesn't require attention-getting devices. He won't overlook what you are doing; he'll reward you well.

Discovery (D): Study Guide For Matthew 6:16-18 – Fasting

Read the passage in the KJV and respond to the following questions:

1. (6:16) What is wrong with the way the "hypocrites" fast? How does this relate to what Jesus has to say about giving and prayer in Matthew 6: 1-15?

2. (6:16) What does the Bible have to say about fasting? (Look up at least six other passages that use this word or phrase – make sure to include Isaiah 58)

3. (6:17-18) What is proper attitude and behavior for fasting? How does this relate to what Jesus has to say about giving and prayer in Matthew 6:1-15?

4. (6:16-18) What is your interpretation and application of this passage?

Explanation (E):

6:16 **WHEN YOU FAST** (*nesteuo*) – In Matthew 6:17, *nesteuo* is a second person plural present subjunctive verb that means the repeated act of fasting. Vine (*Expository Dictionary of N.T. Words*) defines *nesteuo* as "a fasting, fast (from *ne*, a negative prefix, and *esthio*, to eat), is used (a) of voluntary abstinence from food, Luke 2:37; Acts 14:23… fasting had become a common practice among Jews and was continued among Christians: In Acts 27:9, 'the fast' refers to the Day of Atonement, Lev. 16:29… (b) of involuntary abstinence (perhaps voluntary is included), consequent upon trying circumstances, II Cor. 6:5; 11:27." (p. 80)

Barclay (*GOM*, Vol. 1) comments that, "for the Jew, in the time of Jesus, there was only one compulsory fast, the fast of the Day of Atonement. On that day from morning to evening, all men had 'to afflict themselves' (Leviticus 16:31)… Even young children had to be trained to some measure of fasting on the Day of Atonement so that, when they grew up, they would be prepared to accept the national fast. But, although there was only the one compulsory universal day of fasting, the Jews made great use of private fasting." (p. 233)

DO NOT LOOK SOMBER (*skuthropos*) – In Matthew 6:16, *skuthropos* is a nominative plural (subject) of the verb *ginomai* ("to be") which is a second person plural present imperative or present tense command not to look somber when you fast (as the hypocrites do). Vine defines *skuthropos* as "of a sad countenance (*skuthros*, gloomy, sad, *ops*, and eye), is used in Matt. 6:16 and Luke 24:17…" (p. 247)

HYPOCRITES (*hupokrites*) – Vine defines *hupokrites* as "primarily denotes one who answers; then, a stage-actor; it was the custom for Greek and Roman actors to speak in large masks with mechanical devices for augmenting the force of the voice; hence, the word became used metaphorically of a dissembler, a hypocrite." (p. 242)

Barclay (*GOM*, Vol. 1) comments that, "high as the ideal of fasting might be, the practice of it involves certain inevitable dangers. The great danger was that a man might fast as a sign of superior piety, that his fasting might be a deliberate demonstration, not to God, but to men, of how devoted and disciplined a person he was. That is precisely what Jesus was condemning. He was condemning fasting when it was used as an ostentatious parade of piety. The Jewish days of fasting were Monday and Thursday. These were market days, and into the towns and villages, and especially into Jerusalem, there crowded the people from the country; the result was that those who were ostentatiously fasting would on those days have a bigger audience to see and admire their piety. There were many who took deliberate steps to see that others could not miss the fact that they were fasting. They walked through the streets with hair deliberately unkempt and disheveled, with clothes deliberately soiled and disarrayed. They even went to the length of deliberately whitening their faces to accentuate their paleness." (p. 235)

THEY HAVE RECEIVED (*apecho*) – In Matthew 6:16, *apecho* is a third person plural present active indicative verb that means the fact of receiving in full in the present. Note that this is the same verb form as found in Mathew 6:2 and 6:5. Vine defines *apecho* as "to have in full…" (p. 199)

REWARD (*misthos*) – Vine defines *misthos* as "primarily wages, hire, and then, generally, reward…" (p. 294)

6:17 **BUT WHEN YOU FAST** (*nesteuo*) – In Matthew 6:17, *nesteuo* is a nominative singular present participle (verbal adjective) that means the repeated act of fasting. See Matthew 6:16 for definition and description of fasting.

Barclay (*GOM*, Vol. 1) states that, "although Jesus condemned the wrong kind of fasting, his words imply that there is a wise fasting, in which he expected that the Christians would take part. This is a fasting of which few of us ever think… and yet there are many reasons why a wise fasting is an excellent thing. (1) Fasting is good for health… (2) Fasting is good for self-discipline… (3) Fasting preserves us from becoming the slaves of a habit… (4) Fasting preserves the ability to do without things… Fasting makes us appreciate things all the more…" (p. 237-238)

PUT OIL (*aleipho*) – In Matthew 6:17, *aleipho* is a second person singular first aorist middle imperative verb that means the command to put oil on your head at a point in time. Vine defines *aleipho* as "a general term for an anointing of any kind, whether a physical refreshment after washing… or of the sick, Mark 6:13; James 5:14; or a dead body, Mark 16:1. The material used was either oil or ointment…" (p. 58)

WASH (*nipto*) – In Matthew 6:17, *nipto* is a second person singular fist aorist middle imperative verb that means the command to wash your face at a point in time. Vine defines *nipto* as "chiefly used of washing part of the body…" (p. 199)

6:18 **NOT BE OBVIOUS** (*phaino*) – In Matthew 6:18, *phaino* is a second person singular second aorist passive subjunctive verb that means the act of not appearing before men at a point in time without regard for past, present, or future time. Vine defines *phaimo* as "in the Passive, to be brought forth in the light, to become evident, to appear." (p. 64)

FASTING (*nesteuo*) – same verb tense as used in Matthew 6:17 above.

FATHER (*pater*) – Vine defines *pater* as "a nourisher, protector, upholder…" (p. 81)

UNSEEN (*kruptos*) – Vine defines *kruptos* as "secret, hidden (akin to *krupto*, to hide)…" (p. 335)

WHO SEES (*blepo*) – In Matthew 6:18, *blepo* is a nominative singular present active participle that means the ongoing seeing of the unseen by God. Vine defines *blepo* as "to have sight, is used of bodily vision… and mental… It especially stresses the thought of the person who sees." (p. 337)

WILL REWARD YOU (*apodidomi*) – In Matthew 6:18, *apodidomi* is a third person singular future active indicative verb that means the fact of receiving your reward in the future. Vine defines *apodidomi* as "to give up or back, restore, return…" (p. 260)

Bonhoeffer (*The Cost of Discipleship*) comments that, "fasting helps to discipline the self-indulgent and slothful will which is so reluctant to serve the Lord, and it helps to humiliate and chasten the flesh." (p. 188)

See Stott (*SOM*) for a thorough commentary on the purposes of fasting. (p. 135-141)

Application (A):

What insights about discipleship have you gained from this chapter?

While praying through this list of insights, ask God which of these you are already applying and which you need to start applying. Try to identify strengths and weaknesses, and prioritize which weaknesses God wants you to work on.

Identify the top priority issue that God wants you to work on and formulate a study/application plan to allow God to graciously begin his transforming work in your heart. What is God's top priority issue and how are you going to cooperate with him in this?

Is there a mentor or accountability partner who can help you by giving wise counsel, praying, encouraging, holding you accountable, etc.? Who is it and how/when will you contact him/her?

CHAPTER 15

Matthew 6:19-24 – Treasures in Heaven

^{6:19} **Lay not up for yourselves treasures upon earth, where moth and rust doth corrupt, and where thieves break through and steal:** ²⁰ **But lay up for yourselves treasures in heaven, where neither moth nor rust doth corrupt, and where thieves do not break through nor steal:** ²¹ **For where your treasure is, there will your heart be also.** ²² **The light of the body is the eye: if therefore thine eye be single, thy whole body shall be full of light.** ²³ **But if thine eye be evil, thy whole body shall be full of darkness. If therefore the light that is in thee be darkness, how great is that darkness!** ²⁴ **No man can serve two masters: for either he will hate the one, and love the other; or else he will hold to the one, and despise the other. Ye cannot serve God and mammon.** (KJV)

Introduction (I):   Go to biblegateway.com for additional translations and paraphrases.

(NIV)   ^{6:19} "Do not store up for yourselves treasures on earth, where moths and vermin destroy, and where thieves break in and steal. ²⁰ But store up for yourselves treasures in heaven, where moths and vermin do not destroy, and where thieves do not break in and steal. ²¹ For where your treasure is, there your heart will be also. ²² "The eye is the lamp of the body. If your eyes are healthy, your whole body will be full of light. ²³ But if your eyes are unhealthy, your whole body will be full of darkness. If then the light within you is darkness, how great is that darkness! ²⁴ "No one can serve two masters. Either you will hate the one and love the other, or you will be devoted to the one and despise the other. You cannot serve both God and money.

(NASB)   ^{6:19} "Do not store up for yourselves treasures on earth, where moth and rust destroy, and where thieves break in and steal. ²⁰ But store up for yourselves treasures in heaven, where neither moth nor rust destroys, and where thieves do not break in or steal; [21] for where your treasure is, there your heart will be also. [22] "The eye is the lamp of the body; so then if your eye is clear, your whole body will be full of light. [23] But if your eye is bad, your whole body will be full of darkness. If then the light that is in you is darkness, how great is the darkness! [24] "No one can serve two masters; for either he will hate the one and love the other, or he will be devoted to one and despise the other. You cannot serve God and wealth.

(Message) [6:19-21] "Don't hoard treasure down here where it gets eaten by moths and corroded by rust or — worse! — stolen by burglars. Stockpile treasure in heaven, where it's safe from moth and rust and burglars. It's obvious, isn't it? The place where your treasure is, is the place you will most want to be, and end up being. [22-23] "Your eyes are windows into your body. If you open your eyes wide in wonder and belief, your body fills up with light. If you live squinty-eyed in greed and distrust, your body is a dank cellar. If you pull the blinds on your windows, what a dark life you will have! [24] "You can't worship two gods at once. Loving one god, you'll end up hating the other. Adoration of one feeds contempt for the other. You can't worship God and Money both.

Discovery (D): Study Guide For Matthew 6:19-24 – Treasures in Heaven

Read the passage in the KJV and respond to the following questions:

1. (6:19) What does "Lay not up for yourself treasures upon earth" mean? (Look up at least three other passages that use this word or phrase)

2. (6:20) What does "lay up for yourself treasures in heaven" mean? (Look up at least three other passages that use this word or phrase)

3. (6:19-20) What are the contrasts between treasures on earth and treasures in heaven?

4. (6:21) What does "there will your heart be also" mean? (Look up at least three other passages that use this word or phrase)

5. (6:21) How do hearts and treasures relate and what do our treasures tell us about the condition of our heart?

6. (6:22-23) What does "The light of the body is the eye" mean and how does it relate to evil and good?

7. (6:24) What does "No man can serve two masters" mean? (Look up at least three other passages that use this word or phrase)

8. (6:24) What is Jesus teaching about earthly values and heavenly values? How does this relate to the Beatitudes and Salt and Light passages (Matthew 5: 3-16)?

9. (6: 19-24) What is your interpretation and application of this passage?

Explanation (E):

6:19 DO NOT STORE UP (*thesaurizo*) – In Matthew 6:19, *thesaurizo* is a second person plural imperative verb that means the command not to lay up treasures on earth on an ongoing basis. Vine (*Expository Dictionary of N.T. Words*) defines *thesaurizo* as "to lay up, store up (akin to *thesaurus*, a treasury, a storehouse, a treasure), is used of laying up treasures, on earth, Matt. 6:19; in Heaven, ver. 20; in the last days, Jas. 5:3…" (p. 320)

TREASURES (*thesaurus*) – Vine defines *thesaurus* as "(1) a place of safe keeping (possibly akin to *tithemi*, to put), (a) a casket, Matt. 2:11; (b) a storehouse, Matt. 13:42; used metaphorically of the heart, Matt. 12:34… (2) a treasure, Matt. 6:19, 20, 21…" (p. 152)

EARTH (*ge*) – Vine defines *ge* as "(a) earth as arable land, e.g., Matt. 13:5, 8, 23… (b) the earth as a whole, the world, in contrast, whether to the heavens, e.g., Matt. 5:18, 35, or to Heaven, the abode of God, e.g., Matt. 6:19, where the context suggests the earth as a place characterized by mutability and weakness…" (p. 13)

DESTROY (*aphanizo*) – In Matthew 6:19, *aphanizo* is a third person singular present active indicative verb that means the fact of the ongoing process of corruption/corrosion. Vine defines *aphanizo* as "to cause to disappear, put out of sight, came to mean to do away with (*a*, negative, *phaino*, to cause to appear), said of the destructive work of moth and rust, Matt. 6:19, 20…" (p. 232)

STEAL (*klepto*) – In Matthew 6:19, *klepto* is a third person plural present indicative verb that means the fact of ongoing theft of treasures on earth. Vine defines *klepto* as "to steal, akin to *kleptos*, a thief…" (p. 72)

6:20 Parallel structure to verse 6:19 with exception of the command to store up treasures in heaven which will not corrupt or be stolen.

HEAVEN (*ouranos*) – Vine defines *ouranos* as "to lift, to heave…" (p. 208) See Matthew 6:5-15 ("The Lord's Prayer") for further definition of *ouranos*.

6:21 TREASURE IS (*thesaurus*) – *Thesauros* is the object of *eimi* ("to be") and is a third person singular present indicative verb meaning the fact of being a treasure on an ongoing basis.

HEART WILL BE (*kardia*) – *Kardia* is the object of *eimi* ("to be") and is a third person singular future indicative verb meaning the fact of our heart following after the values of our treasures.

6:22 **EYE** (*ophthalmos*) – Vine defines *ophthalmos* as "akin to *opsis*, sight, probably from a root signifying penetration, sharpness… (a) of the physical organ, e.g., Matt. 5:38… (b) metaphorically, of ethical qualities, evil, Matt. 6:23… (c) metaphorically, of mental vision, Matt. 13:15…" (p. 64)

IS THE LAMP (*lampas*) – *Lampas* is the object of *eimi* ("to be") and is a third person singular present indicative verb that means the fact of being light of the body on an ongoing basis. Vine defines *lampas* as "a torch (akin to *lamp*, to shine), frequently fed, like a lamp, with oil from a little vessel used for the purpose (the *angeion* of Matt. 25:4); they held a little oil and would frequently need replenishing." (p. 307-308)

BODY (*soma*) – Vine defines *soma* as "the body as a whole, the instrument of life…" (p. 136)

GOOD (*haplous*) – *Haplous* is the object of *eimi* ("to be") and is a third person singular present subjunctive verb that means the repeated or ongoing singleness of the eye. Vine defines *haplous* as "simple, single, is used in a moral sense in Matt. 6:22 and Luke 11:34, said of the eye; singleness of purpose keeps us from the snare of having a double treasure and consequently a divided heart." (p. 35)

FULL OF LIGHT (*phos*) – *Phos* is the object of *eimi* ("to be") and is a third person singular future indicative verb that means the fact of being light in the future. Vine defines *phos* as "akin to *phao*, to give light (from roots *pha-* and *phan-*, expressing light as seen by the eye, and metaphorically as reaching the mind, whence *phaino*, to make to appear, *phaneros*, evident)…" (p. 339-340)

6:23 Parrallel structure to verse 6:22 with same verb tenses used.

BAD (*poneros*) – Vine defines *poneros* as "akin to *ponos*, labor, toil, denotes evil that causes labor, pain, sorrow, malignant evil…" (p. 50)

DARKNESS (*skotia*) – Vine defines *skotia* as "full of darkness, or covered with darkness… The group of *skot*-words is derived from a root *ska-*, meaning to cover. The same root is to be found in *skene*, a tent." (p. 267)

GREAT (*posos*) – Vine defines *posos* as "how much, how great, how many…" (p. 41)

6:24 **SERVE** (*douleuo*) – In Matthew 6:24, *douleuo* is a present infinitive (verbal noun) that means the ongoing act of serving. Vine defines *douleuo* as "from *deo*, to bind, a slave, originally the lowest term in the scale of servitude, came also to mean one who gives himself up to the will of another, e.g., I Cor. 7:23; Rom. 6:17, 20, and became the most common and general word for 'servant,' as in Matt. 8:9, without any idea of bondage." (p. 139)

MASTERS (*kurios*) – Vine defines *kurios* as "a lord, one who exercises power..." (p. 46)

HATE (*miseo*) – In Matthew 6:24, *miseo* is a third person singular future active indicative verb that means the fact of hating in the future. Vine defines *miseo* as "malicious and unjustifiable feelings towards others, whether towards the innocent or by mutual animosity..." (p. 198)

LOVE (*agapao*) – In Matthew 6:24, *agapao* is a third person singular future verb that means loving in the future. See Matthew 5:43-48 ("Love for Enemies") for definition and description of *agapao*.

DEVOTED (*antecho*) – In Matthew 6:24, *antecho* is a third person singular future verb that means loving devotion in the future. Vine defines *antecho* as "*anti*, against, or... signifies in the Middle Voice, (a) to hold firmly to, cleave to, of holding or cleaving to a person, Matt. 6:24..." (p. 224)

DESPISE (*kataphroneo*) – In Matthew 6:24, *kataphroneo* is a third person singular future indicative that means the fact that a person will despise the other in the future. Vine defines *kataphroneo* as "to think down upon or against anyone (*kata*, down, *phren*, the mind), hence signifies to think slightly of, to despise, Matt. 6:24..." (p. 301)

MAMMOM (*mamonas*) – Vine defines *mamonas* as "a common Aramaic word for riches, akin to a Hebrew word signifying to be firm, steadfast (*Amen*), hence, that which is to be trusted..." (p. 32)

See Stott (*SOM*) for excellent commentary on materialism (p. 153-159)

Application (A):

What insights about discipleship have you gained from this chapter?

While praying through this list of insights, ask God which of these you are already applying and which you need to start applying. Try to identify strengths and weaknesses, and prioritize which weaknesses God wants you to work on.

Identify the top priority issue that God wants you to work on and formulate a study/application plan to allow God to graciously begin his transforming work in your heart. What is God's top priority issue and how are you going to cooperate with him in this?

Is there a mentor or accountability partner who can help you by giving wise counsel, praying, encouraging, holding you accountable, etc.? Who is it and how/when will you contact him/her?

CHAPTER 16

Matthew 6:25-34 – Seek the Kingdom

^{6:25} Therefore I say unto you, Take no thought for your life, what ye shall eat, or what ye shall drink; nor yet for your body, what ye shall put on. Is not the life more than meat, and the body than raiment? ²⁶ Behold the fowls of the air: for they sow not, neither do they reap, nor gather into barns; yet your heavenly Father feedeth them. Are ye not much better than they? ²⁷ Which of you by taking thought can add one cubit unto his stature? ²⁸ And why take ye thought for raiment? Consider the lilies of the field, how they grow; they toil not, neither do they spin: ²⁹ And yet I say unto you, That even Solomon in all his glory was not arrayed like one of these. ³⁰ Wherefore, if God so clothe the grass of the field, which to day is, and to morrow is cast into the oven, shall he not much more clothe you, O ye of little faith? ³¹ Therefore take no thought, saying, What shall we eat? or, What shall we drink? or, Wherewithal shall we be clothed? ³² (For after all these things do the Gentiles seek:) for your heavenly Father knoweth that ye have need of all these things. ³³ But seek ye first the kingdom of God, and his righteousness; and all these things shall be added unto you. ³⁴ Take therefore no thought for the morrow: for the morrow shall take thought for the things of itself. Sufficient unto the day is the evil thereof. (KJV)

Introduction (I): Go to biblegateway.com for additional translations and paraphrases.

(NIV)   ^{6:25} "Therefore I tell you, do not worry about your life, what you will eat or drink; or about your body, what you will wear. Is not life more than food, and the body more than clothes? ²⁶ Look at the birds of the air; they do not sow or reap or store away in barns, and yet your heavenly Father feeds them. Are you not much more valuable than they? ²⁷ Can any one of you by worrying add a single hour to your life? ²⁸ "And why do you worry about clothes? See how the flowers of the field grow. They do not labor or spin. ²⁹ Yet I tell you that not even Solomon in all his splendor was dressed like one of these. [30] If that is how God clothes the grass of the field, which is here today and tomorrow is thrown into the fire, will he not much more clothe you—you of little faith? [31] So do not worry, saying, 'What shall we eat?' or 'What shall we drink?' or 'What shall we wear?' [32] For the pagans run after all these things, and your heavenly Father knows that you need them. [33] But seek first his kingdom and his righteousness, and all these things will be given to you as well. [34] Therefore do not worry about tomorrow, for tomorrow will worry about itself. Each day has enough trouble of its own.

(NASB) [6:25] "For this reason I say to you, [do not be worried about your life, as to what you will eat or what you will drink; nor for your body, as to what you will put on. Is not life more than food, and the body more than clothing? [26] Look at the birds of the air, that they do not sow, nor reap nor gather into barns, and yet your heavenly Father feeds them. Are you not worth much more than they? [27] And who of you by being worried can add a single hour to his life? [28] And why are you worried about clothing? Observe how the lilies of the field grow; they do not toil nor do they spin, [29] yet I say to you that not even Solomon in all his glory clothed himself like one of these. [30] But if God so clothes the grass of the field, which is alive today and tomorrow is thrown into the furnace, will He not much more clothe you? You of little faith! [31] Do not worry then, saying, 'What will we eat?' or 'What will we drink?' or 'What will we wear for clothing?' [32] For the Gentiles eagerly seek all these things; for your heavenly Father knows that you need all these things. [33] But seek first His kingdom and His righteousness, and all these things will be added to you. [34] "So do not worry about tomorrow; for tomorrow will care for itself. Each day has enough trouble of its own.

(Message) [6:25-26] "If you decide for God, living a life of God-worship, it follows that you don't fuss about what's on the table at mealtimes or whether the clothes in your closet are in fashion. There is far more to your life than the food you put in your stomach, more to your outer appearance than the clothes you hang on your body. Look at the birds, free and unfettered, not tied down to a job description, careless in the care of God. And you count far more to him than birds. [27-29] "Has anyone by fussing in front of the mirror ever gotten taller by so much as an inch? All this time and money wasted on fashion—do you think it makes that much difference? Instead of looking at the fashions, walk out into the fields and look at the wildflowers. They never primp or shop, but have you ever seen color and design quite like it? The ten best-dressed men and women in the country look shabby alongside them. ³⁰⁻³³ "If God gives such attention to the appearance of wildflowers—most of which are never even seen—don't you think he'll attend to you, take pride in you, do his best for you? What I'm trying to do here is to get you to relax, to not be so preoccupied with getting, so you can respond to God's giving. People who don't know God and the way he works fuss over these things, but you know both God and how he works. Steep your life in God-reality, God-initiative, God-provisions. Don't worry about missing out. You'll find all your everyday human concerns will be met. ³⁴ "Give your entire attention to what God is doing right now, and don't get worked up about what may or may not happen tomorrow. God will help you deal with whatever hard things come up when the time comes.

Discovery (D): Study Guide for Matthew 6:25-34 – Seek the Kingdom

Read the passage in the KJV and respond to the following questions:

1. (6:25) What does "Take no thought [worry] for your life" mean? (Look up at least three other passages that use this word or phrase – include Philippians 4: 4-9)

2. (6:25) What does "Is not the life more than meat, and the body than raiment [clothes]" mean? How does this relate to Jesus' teaching on treasures in Matthew 6:24?

3. (6:26- 32) What is Jesus trying to illustrate in these verses (related to verse 25)?

4. (6:32) What does "your heavenly Father knoweth that ye have need of all these things" mean?

5. (6:33) What does "But seek ye first the kingdom of God" mean? (Look up at least three other passages that use this word or phrase)

6. (6:33) How do the kingdom and "righteousness" relate? (See Matthew 5:6)

7. (6:33) What does "all these things will be added onto you" mean? (Look up at least three other passages that use this word or phrase – make sure to include Philippians 4:4-9)

8. (6:34) What does "Take no thought [worry] for the morrow" mean? How is this possible? (Compare this with Matthew 6:25)

9. (6:25-34) What is your interpretation and application of this passage?

Explanation (E):

6:25 **DO NOT WORRY** (*merimnao*) – In Matthew 6:25, *merimnao* is a second person plural present imperative verb that means the command to not be anxious on an ongoing basis. Vine (*Expository Dictionary of N.T. Words*) defines *merimnao* as "probably connected to *merizo*, to draw in different directions, distract, hence signifies that which causes this, a care, especially an anxious care, Matt. 13:22; Mark 4:19…" (p. 168)

LIFE (*psuche*) – Vine defines *psuche* as "besides its meanings, heart, mind, soul, denotes life in two chief respects, (a) breath of life, the natural life, e.g., Matt. 2:20; 6:25… (b) the seat of personality, e.g., Luke 9:24…" (p. 337)

EAT (*phago*) – In Matthew 6:25, *phago* is a second person plural second aorist subjunctive verb that means the completed act of eating at a point in time. Vine defines *phago* as "to eat, devour, consume…" (p. 15)

DRINK (*pino*) – same verb tense as *phago* above. Vine defines *pino* as "to drink…" (p. 339)

WEAR (*enduro*) – In Matthew 6:25, *enduo* is a second person plural first aorist middle subjunctive verb that means the act of putting on clothes at a point in time. Vine defines *enduo* as "used in the Middle Vocie, of putting on oneself, or an another…" (p. 236)

MORE IMPORTANT (*pleion*) – Vine defines *pleion* as "the comparative degree of *polus*, much…" (p. 82)

6:26 **LOOK** (*emblepo*) – In Matthew 6:26, *emblepo* is a second person plural first aorist imperative that means the command to take a complete look. Vine defines *emblepo* as "to look at (*en*, in, *blepo*, to see), is translated to look upon in Mark 10:27… This verb implies a close, penetrating look…" (p. 13)

FATHER (*pater*) – Vine defines *pater* as "a nourisher, protector, upholder…" (p. 81)

FEEDS THEM (*trepho*) – In Matthew 5:26, *trepho* is a third person singular present active indicative verb that means the fact of God supplying them with food on an ongoing basis. Vine defines *trepho* as "to nourish, feed, Matt. 6:26… of a mother, to give suck, Luke 23:29… to fatten, as of fattening animals, Jas. 5:5…" (p. 88)

MORE VALUABLE (*diaphero*) – In Matthew 6:26, *diaphero* is a second person plural indicative verb that means the fact of being more valuable on an ongoing basis. Vine defines *diaphero* as "(*dia*, through, *phero*, to carry)… to excel, be better. e.g., Matt. 6:26…" (p. 122)

6:27 **WORRYING** (*merimnao*) – In Matthew 6:27, *merimnao* is a nominative singular present participle that means ongoing worrying. See Matthew 6:25 for definition of *merimnao*.

ADD (*prostithemi*) – In Matthew 6:27, *prostithemi* is a second aorist active infinitive (vebal noun) that means the complete act of adding at a point in time. Vine defines *prostithemi* as "to put to (*pros*, to, *tithemi*, to put), to add, or to place beside…" (p. 29)

6:28–30 **WORRY** (*merimnao*) – In Matthew 6:28, *merimnao* is a second person plural present indicative verb that means the fact of worrying on an ongoing basis. See Matthew 6:25 for definition of *merimnao*.

LITTLE FAITH (*oligopistos*) – In Matthew 6:30, *oligopistos* is a masculine plural vocative (direct address). Vine defines *oligopistos* as "little faith (*oligos*, little, *pistis*, faith), is used only of the Lord, and as a tender rebuke, for anxiety, Matt. 6:30 and Luke 13:28; for fear, Matt. 8:26; 14:31; 16:8." (p. 72)

6:31-32 **DO NOT WORRY** (*merimnao*) – In Matthew 6:31, *merimnao* is a second person plural first aorist subjunctive verb that means the act of worrying at a point in time. See Matthew 6:25 for definition and description of *merimnao*.

PAGANS (*ethnos*) – Vine defines *ethnos* as "'heathen,'… a multitude or company; then a multitude of people of the same nature or genus, a nation, people…" (p. 144)

RUN AFTER (*epizeteo*) – In Matthew 6:32, *epizeteo* is a third person plural present active indicative verb that means the fact of seeking after on an ongoing basis. Vine defines *epizeteo* as "to seek after (directive, *epi*, towards), is always rendered in the R.V., by some form of the verb to seek…" (p. 340)

KNOWS (*oida*) – In Matthew 6:32, *oida* is a third person singular verb. Vine defines *oida* as "a perfect tense with a present meaning, signifying, primarily, to have seen or perceived; hence, to know, to have knowledge of…" (p. 298)

NEED (*chrezo*) – In Matthew 6:32, *chrezo* is a second person plural present indicative verb that means the fact of ongoing need. Vine defines *chrezo* as "to need, to have need of (akin to *chre*, it is necessary, fitting)…" (p. 106)

6:33 SEEK FIRST (*zeteo/protos*) – In Matthew 6:33, *zeteo* is a second person plural present active imperative verb that means the command to seek and keep on seeking after God's kingdom and His righteousness. Vine defines *zeteo* as "to seek, to seek for…" (p. 339) Vine defines *protos* ("first") as "the superlative degree of *pro*, before…" (p. 103)

KINGDOM (*basiliea*)/**RIGHTEOUSNESS** (*dikaiosune*) – See Matthew 5:3 ("Poor in Spirit") and 5:6 ("Hunger and Thirst After Righteousness") for definitions and descriptions.

WILL BE GIVEN TO YOU (*prostithemi*) – In Matthew 6:33, *prostithemi* is a third person singular future passive indicative verb that means the fact that God will give us all we need in the future if we seek Him first. Vine defines *prostithemi* as "to put to (*pros*, to, *tithemi*, to put), to add, or to place beside…" (p. 29)

6:34 DO NOT WORRY (*merimnao*) – same verb tense as verse 6:31 above.

WILL WORRY ABOUT ITSELF (*merimnao*) – In Matthew 6:34, *merimnao* is a third person singular future indicative verb that the means the fact of worry in the future. See Matthew 6:31 for definition of *merimnaeo*.

ENOUGH (*arketos*) – Vine defines *arketos* as "to ward off; hence, to aid, assist; then, to be strong enough, i.e., to suffice, to be enough…" (p. 32)

TROUBLE (*kakos*) – Vine defines *kakos* as "for whatever is evil in character, base, in distinction from *poneros*… which indicates what is evil in influence and effect, malignant. *Kakos* is the wider term and often covers the meaning of *poneros*. *Kakos* is antithetic to *kalos*, fair, advisable, good in character, and to, beneficial, useful, good in act; hence it denotes what is useless, incapable, bad…" (p. 50)

Lloyd-Jones (*Sermon on the Mount*) states that, "Nothing seems to be more natural to mankind in this world than to become anxious, to become burdened and worried... He [Jesus] says in effect, 'Wait a minute; consider this before you become anxious. Is not your life more than meat, the sustenance, the food?... What does the Lord mean by this?... I need never to be concerned or worried or anxious that suddenly there will not be sufficient to keep this life of mine going. That will never happen to me; it is impossible. If God has given me the gift of life, He will see to it that life is kept going." (p. 112-113)

Barclay (*GOM*, Vol. 1) comments that, "Jesus says that worry can be defeated when we acquire the art of living one day at a time (verse 34). The Jews had a saying: 'Do not worry over tomorrow's evils, for you do not know what today will bring forth. Perhaps tomorrow you will not be alive, and you will have worried for a world which will not be yours.' If each day is lived as it comes, if each task is done as it appears, then the sum of all the days is bound to be good. It is Jesus' advise that we should handle the demands of each day as it comes, without worrying about the unknown future and the things which may never happen." (p. 289) Barclay states that we can live like this because of God's sufficiency, "Those of steadfast mind you keep in peace – in peace because they trust in you (Isaiah 6:3)." (p. 301)

Application (A):

What insights about discipleship have you gained from this chapter?

While praying through this list of insights, ask God which of these you are already applying and which you need to start applying. Try to identify strengths and weaknesses, and prioritize which weaknesses God wants you to work on.

Identify the top priority issue that God wants you to work on and formulate a study/application plan to allow God to graciously begin his transforming work in your heart. What is God's top priority issue and how are you going to cooperate with him in this?

Is there a mentor or accountability partner who can help you by giving wise counsel, praying, encouraging, holding you accountable, etc.? Who is it and how/when will you contact him/her?

CHAPTER 17

Matthew 7:1-6 – Judging

^{7:1} Judge not, that ye be not judged. ² For with what judgment ye judge, ye shall be judged: and with what measure ye mete, it shall be measured to you again. ³ And why beholdest thou the mote that is in thy brother's eye, but considerest not the beam that is in thine own eye? ⁴ Or how wilt thou say to thy brother, Let me pull out the mote out of thine eye; and, behold, a beam is in thine own eye? ⁵ Thou hypocrite, first cast out the beam out of thine own eye; and then shalt thou see clearly to cast out the mote out of thy brother's eye. ⁶ Give not that which is holy unto the dogs, neither cast ye your pearls before swine, lest they trample them under their feet, and turn again and rend you. (KJV)

Introduction (I): Go to biblegateway.com for additional translations and paraphrases.

(NIV) ^{7:1} "Do not judge, or you too will be judged. ² For in the same way you judge others, you will be judged, and with the measure you use, it will be measured to you. ³ "Why do you look at the speck of sawdust in your brother's eye and pay no attention to the plank in your own eye? ⁴ How can you say to your brother, 'Let me take the speck out of your eye,' when all the time there is a plank in your own eye? ⁵ You hypocrite, first take the plank out of your own eye, and then you will see clearly to remove the speck from your brother's eye. ⁶ "Do not give dogs what is sacred; do not throw your pearls to pigs. If you do, they may trample them under their feet, and turn and tear you to pieces.

(NASB) ^{7:1} "Do not judge so that you will not be judged. ² For in the way you judge, you will be judged; and by your standard of measure, it will be measured to you. ³ Why do you look at the speck that is in your brother's eye, but do not notice the log that is in your own eye? ⁴ Or how can you say to your brother, 'Let me take the speck out of your eye,' and behold, the log is in

your own eye? [5] You hypocrite, first take the log out of your own eye, and then you will see clearly to take the speck out of your brother's eye.
[6] "Do not give what is holy to dogs, and do not throw your pearls before swine, or they will trample them under their feet, and turn and tear you to pieces.

(Message) [7:1-5] "Don't pick on people, jump on their failures, criticize their faults—unless, of course, you want the same treatment. That critical spirit has a way of boomeranging. It's easy to see a smudge on your neighbor's face and be oblivious to the ugly sneer on your own. Do you have the nerve to say, 'Let me wash your face for you,' when your own face is distorted by contempt? It's this whole traveling road-show mentality all over again, playing a holier-than-thou part instead of just living your part. Wipe that ugly sneer off your own face, and you might be fit to offer a washcloth to your neighbor. [6] "Don't be flip with the sacred. Banter and silliness give no honor to God. Don't reduce holy mysteries to slogans. In trying to be relevant, you're only being cute and inviting sacrilege.

Discovery (D): Study Guide for Matthew 7:1-6 – Judging

Read the passage in the KJV and respond to the following questions:

1. (7:1) What does "Don't judge other people" mean? (Look up at least three other passages that use this word or phrase)

2. (7:1-2) What does "that ye not be judged" mean? What is the relationship between judging others and being judged? (Compare this with forgiveness in Matthew 6: 12, 14-15)

3. (7:3-5) What does "mote [speck]… beam" mean? Why does Jesus call this type of person a "hypocrite"?

4. (7:5) What does this passage have to teach us about the source of being judgmental and how to become less so?

5. (7:6) What does "Give not that which is holy unto the dogs" mean? How does this relate to taking the "mote" out of someone else's eye (verse 5)?

6. (7:1-6) What is your interpretation and application of this passage?

Explanation (E):

7:1 **DO NOT JUDGE** (*krino*) – In Matthew 7:1, *krino* is a second person plural present active imperative verb that means the command to not go on judging. Vine (*Expository Dictionary of N.T. Words*) defines *krino* as "primarily denotes to separate, select, choose; hence, to determine, and so to judge, pronounce judgment." (p. 280) Kittle (*Theological*

Dictionary of the N.T.) defines *krino* as "the N.T. sense is usually 'to judge' with God or man as subject and in either an official or a personal sense." (p. 469)

YOU TOO WILL BE JUDGED (*krino*) – In Matthew 7:1, *krino* is a second person plural first aorist passive subjunctive verb that means to be judged at a pointing time regardless of past, present, or future time.

6:2 **SAME WAY** - Literally means "with what for."

JUDGING OTHERS (*krino*) – In Matthew 7:2, *krino* is a second person plural present active indicative verb that means the fact of judging others on an ongoing basis. See definition of *krino* in verse 7:1 above.

WILL BE JUDGED (*krino*) – In Matthew 7:2, *krino* is a second person plural future passive verb that means that judgment will come in the future.

MEASURE YOU USE (*metreo*) – In Matthew 7:2, *metreo* is a second person plural present active indicative verb that means the ongoing fact of measuring. Vine defines *metreo* as "to measure… (a) of space, number, value, etc., Rev. 11:1, 2… (b) in the sense of measuring out, giving by measure, Matt. 7:2…" (p. 53)

WILL BE MEASURED (*metreo*) – In Matthew 7:2, *metreo* is a third person singular future passive indicative verb that means the fact of receiving the measure that we measured out in the future.

7:3 **LOOK** (*blepo*) – In Matthew 7:3, *blepo* is a second person singular present active indicative verb that means the fact of looking on an ongoing basis. Vine defines *blepo* as "(a) bodily and (b) mental vision… indicates greater vividness than *horao*, expressing a more intent, earnest, contemplation…" (p. 114)

SPECK OF SAWDUST (*karphos*) – Vine defines *karphos* as "a small, dry stalk, a twig, a bit of dried stick (from *karpho*, to dry up), or a tiny straw or bit of wool, such as might fly into the eye, is used metaphorically of a minor fault, Matt. 7:3, 4, 5; Luke 6:41, 42 (twice), in contrast with *dokos*, a beam supporting the roof of a building…" (p. 85)

BROTHER (*adelphos*) – Vine defines *adelphos* as "a brother, or near kinsman; in the plural, a community based on identity of origin or life." (p. 154)

PAY NO ATTENTION (*katamanthano*) – In Matthew 7:3, *katamanthano* is a second person singular present indicative verb that means the ongoing fact of not paying attention.

Vine defines *katamanthano* as "to learn thoroughly (*kata*, down, intensive, *manthano*, to learn), hence, to note accurately, consider well…" (p. 230)

PLANK (*dokos*) – Vine defines *dokos* as "a beam, is perhaps etymologically connected with the root *dek-*, seen in the word *dechomai*, to receive, beams being received at their ends into walls or pieces of timber." (p. 100)

7:4 **HOW CAN YOU SAY** (*eiro*) – In Matthew 7:4, *eiro* is a second person singular future indicative verb that means the fact of saying in the future. Vine defines *eiro* as "an obsolete verb, has the future tense *ereo*, e.g., Matt. 7:4…" (p. 324)

BROTHER (*adelphos*) – See verse 7:3 for definition of *adelphos*.

LET ME TAKE (*ekballo*) – In Matthew 7:4, *ekballo* is a first person singular second aorist active subjunctive verb that means to take out something at a point in time without reference to the past, present, or future. Vine defines *ekballo* as "to cast out of, from, forth…" (p. 172)

SPECK (*karphos*) – See verse 7:3 for definition of *karphos*.

ALL THE TIME (*idou*) – Vine defines *idou* as "to see, calling attention to what may be seen or heard or mentally apprehended in any way." (p. 114)

PLANK (*dokos*) – See verse 7:3 for definition of *dokos*.

7:5 **HYPOCRITE** (*hupokrites*) – Vine defines *hupokrites* as "one who answers; then, a stage-actor; it was a custom for Greek and Roman actors to speak in large masks with mechanical devices for augmenting the force of the voice; hence the word became used metaphorically of a dissembler, a hypocrite." (p. 242)

TAKE THE PLANK OUT (*ekballo*) – In Matthew 7:5, *ekballo* is a second person singular second aorist active imperative verb that means the command to take something out at a point in time. See verse 7:4 for definition of *ekballo*.

PLANK (*dokos*) – See verse 7:3 for definition of *dokos*.

YOU WILL SEE CLEARLY (*diablepo*) – In Matthew 7:5, *diablepo* is a second person singular future indicative verb that means the fact of seeing clearly in the future because you have plucked out the beam in your own eye. Vine defines *diablepo* as "to see clearly (*dia*, through, *blepo*, to have sight)…" (p. 337)

TO REMOVE (*ekballo*) – In Matthew 7:5, *ekballo* is a second aorist active infinitive (verbal noun) that means removing something at a point in time. See Matthew 7:4 for definition of *ekballo*.

SPECK (*karphos*) – See verse 7:3 for definition of *karphos*.

7:6 **DO NOT GIVE** (*didomai*) – In Matthew 7:6, *didomai* is a second person plural second aorist active subjunctive verb that means to give at a point in time without reference to past, present, or future time. Vine defines *didomai* as "to give… the implied idea being that of giving freely." (p.121)

DOGS (*kuon*) – Vine defines *kuon* as "used in two senses, (a) natural, Matt. 7:6… (b) metaphorically, Phil. 3:2… of those whose moral impurity will exclude them from the New Jerusalem. The Jews used the term of Gentiles, under the idea of ceremonial impurity. Among the Greeks it was an epithet of imprudence." (p. 332)

SACRED (*hagios*) – Vine defines *hagios* as "fundamentally signifies separated (among the Greeks, dedicated to the gods), and hence, in Scripture in its moral and spiritual significance, separated from sin and therefore consecrated to God, sacred." (p. 226)

DO NOT THROW (*ballo*) – Same verb tense and construction as phrase above.

THEY MAY TRAMPLE (*katapateo*) – In Matthew 7:6, *katapateo* is a third person plural first aorist active subjunctive verb that means the trampling at a point in time. Vine defines *katapatereo* as "to tread down, to trample under foot…" (p. 148)

TEAR YOU (*rhegnumi*) – In Matthew 7:6, *rhegnumi* is a third person plural first aorist active subjunctive verb that means tearing at a point in time. Vine defines *rhegnumi* as "to tear, rend…" (p. 277)

Carson (*The Sermon on the Mount*) concludes that, "'to judge' can mean to discern, to judge judicially, to be judgmental, to condemn (judicially or otherwise). The context must determine the precise shade of meaning. The context here argues that the verse means, "Do not be judgmental.' Do not adopt a critical spirit, a condemning attitude." (p. 99)

Lloyd-Jones (*The Sermon on the Mount*) states that, "Our Lord tells us that we must not judge in the sense of condemning; but He reminds us here that that is not the total statement with regard to this matter… The simple answer ["perfect balance"] is that, while our Lord exhorts us not to be hypercritical, He never tells us not to be discriminating. There is an absolute difference between these two things. What we are to avoid is the tendency to be censorious, to condemn people, to set ourselves up as the final judge and to make a pronouncement on persons. But that, of course, is very different from exercising a spirit of discrimination [discernment], to which the Scripture is ever exhorting us." (p. 183-184)

Application (A):

What insights about discipleship have you gained from this chapter?

While praying through this list of insights, ask God which of these you are already applying and which you need to start applying. Try to identify strengths and weaknesses, and prioritize which weaknesses God wants you to work on.

Identify the top priority issue that God wants you to work on and formulate a study/application plan to allow God to graciously begin his transforming work in your heart. What is God's top priority issue and how are you going to cooperate with him in this?

Is there a mentor or accountability partner who can help you by giving wise counsel, praying, encouraging, holding you accountable, etc.? Who is it and how/when will you contact him/her?

CHAPTER 18

Matthew 7:7-12 – Ask, Seek, Knock

7:7 Ask, and it shall be given you; seek, and ye shall find; knock, and it shall be opened unto you: **8** For every one that asketh receiveth; and he that seeketh findeth; and to him that knocketh it shall be opened. **9** Or what man is there of you, whom if his son ask bread, will he give him a stone? **10** Or if he ask a fish, will he give him a serpent? **11** If ye then, being evil, know how to give good gifts unto your children, how much more shall your Father which is in heaven give good things to them that ask him? **12** Therefore all things whatsoever ye would that men should do to you, do ye even so to them: for this is the law and the prophets. (KJV)

Introduction (I): Go to biblegateway.com for additional translations and paraphrases.

(NIV) **7:7** "Ask and it will be given to you; seek and you will find; knock and the door will be opened to you. **8** For everyone who asks receives; the one who seeks finds; and to the one who knocks, the door will be opened. **9** "Which of you, if your son asks for bread, will give him a stone? **10** Or if he asks for a fish, will give him a snake? **11** If you, then, though you are evil, know how to give good gifts to your children, how much more will your Father in heaven give good gifts to those who ask him! **12** So in everything, do to others what you would have them do to you, for this sums up the Law and the Prophets.

(NASB) **7:7** "Ask, and it will be given to you; seek, and you will find; knock, and it will be opened to you. **8** For everyone who asks receives, and he who seeks finds, and to him who knocks it will be opened. **9** Or what man is there among you who, when his son asks for a loaf, will give him a stone? **10** Or if he asks for a fish, he will not give him a snake, will he? **11** If you then, being evil, know how to give good gifts to your children, how much more will your Father who is in heaven give what is good to those who ask Him!

[12] "In everything, therefore, treat people the same way you want them to treat you, for this is the Law and the Prophets.

(Message) [7:7-11] "Don't bargain with God. Be direct. Ask for what you need. This isn't a cat-and-mouse, hide-and-seek game we're in. If your child asks for bread, do you trick him with sawdust? If he asks for fish, do you scare him with a live snake on his plate? As bad as you are, you wouldn't think of such a thing. You're at least decent to your own children. So don't you think the God who conceived you in love will be even better? [12] "Here is a simple, rule-of-thumb guide for behavior: Ask yourself what you want people to do for you, then grab the initiative and do it for them. Add up God's Law and Prophets and this is what you get.

Discovery (D): Study Guide for Matthew 7:7-12 – Ask, Seek, Knock

Read the passage in the KJV and respond to the following questions:

1. (7:7) What does "Ask… seek… knock" mean? (The tense of these words is present active indicative meaning a command to ask, and keep on asking… etc.)

2. (7:7-10) What happens if the follower of Christ is faithful and persistent in asking, seeking, and knocking? (See Matthew 6: 33; Luke 11: 5-14 and 18: 1-8)

3. (7:11) What contrasts does Jesus make in comparing the characteristics of an "evil" father and our "heavenly Father"? Why is this important?

4. (7:12) What does "whatsoever ye would that men should do to you, do ye even so to them" mean? (Compare this with the "Great Commandment in Matthew 22:34-40; the "New Commandment" in John 13:34-35; and "bearing one another's burdens" in Galatians 6:1-5)

5. (7:12) How does "doing onto others" (Golden Rule) sum up "the Law and the Prophets"? How does this relate to not being judgmental of others (verse 1) and asking, seeking, and knocking (verse 7)?

6. (7:7-12) What is your interpretation and application of this passage?

Explanation (E):

7:7 **ASK** (*aiteo*) – In Matthew 7:7, *aiteo* is a second person plural present active imperative verb that means the command to ask and keep on asking. Vine (*Expository Dictionary of the N.T.*) defines *aiteo* as "the attitude of a suppliant, the petition of one who is lesser in position than he to whom the petition is made…" (p. 79)

Barclay (*GOM*, Vol. 1) comments that, "In the Greek, there are two kinds of imperative: there is the *aorist* imperative, which issues one definite command [i.e. "Shut the door!"]… There is the *present* imperative, which issues a command that a person should always do something or should go on doing something [i.e. "Always, keep on shutting doors behind you!"]. The imperatives here are present imperatives; therefore Jesus is saying: 'Go on asking; go on seeking; go on knocking.' He is telling us to persist in prayer; he is telling us to never be discouraged in prayer. Clearly, therein lies the test of our sincerity. Do we really want a thing ["in his way"]…" (p. 314)

WILL BE GIVEN (*didomai*) – In Matthew 7:7, *didomai* is a third person singular future passive indicative verb that means the fact of being given something at a future time.

SEEK (*zeteo*) – In Matthew 7:7, *zeteo* is a second person plural present active imperative verb that means the command to seek and keep on seeking.

WILL FIND (*heurisko*) – In Matthew 7:7, *heurisko* is a third person singular future active indicative verb that means the fact of finding something in the future.

KNOCK (*krouo*) – In Matthew 7:7, *krouo* is a second personal plural present active imperative verb that means the command to knock and keep on knocking.

WILL BE OPENED (*anoigo*) – In Matthew 7:7, *anoigo* is a third person singular future passive indicative verb that means the fact of the door being opened at a future point in time.

7:8 **ASKS** (*aiteo*) – In Matthew 7:8, *aiteo* is a nominative singular present active participle that means the act of ongoing asking.

RECEIVES (*lambano*) – In Matthew 7:8, *lambano* is a third person singular present active indicative verb that means the fact of receiving on an ongoing basis.

SEEKS (*zeteo*) – In Matthew 7:8, *zeteo* is a nominative singular present active participle that means the act of ongoing seeking.

FINDS (*heurisko*) – In Matthew 7:8, *heurisko* is a third person singular present active indicative verb that means the fact of finding on an ongoing basis.

KNOCKS (*krouo*) – In Matthew 7:8, *krouo* is a dative singular present participle that means the ongoing act of knocking.

OPENED (*anoigo*) – In Matthew 7:8, *anoigo* is a third person singular future passive verb that means that the door is opened at a future point in time.

Barclay (*GOM*, Vol. 1) comments that, "there is a lesson here: God will always answer our prayers; *but he will answer them in his way*, and his way will be the way of perfect wisdom and of perfect love." (p. 313)

7:9-10 Barclay (*GOM*, Vol. 1) comments that, "Jesus' examples are carefully chosen. He takes three examples, for Luke adds a third to the two Matthew gives. If a son asks for bread, will his father give him a stone? If a son asks for a fish, will his father give him a serpent? If a son asks for an egg, will his father give him a scorpion? (Luke 11:12)" (p. 271) Barclay continues, "Jesus' argument is very simple. One of the Jewish Rabbis asked, 'Is there a man who ever hates his son?' Jesus' argument is that no father ever refused the request of his son; and God the great Father will never refuse the request of his children." (p. 270)

7:11 **EVIL** (*poneros*) – Vine defines *poneros* as "akin to *ponos*, labor, toil, denotes evil that causes labor, pain, sorrow, malignant evil…" (p. 50)

GIVE (*didomai*) – In Matthew 7:11, *didomai* is a present active infinitive that means ongoing giving.

GOOD GIFTS (*agathos*) – Vine defines *agathos* as "being good in its character or constitution, is beneficial in its effect…" (p. 163)

MUCH MORE (*mallon*) – Vine defines *mallon* as "the comparative degree of *mala*, very, very much…" (p. 81)

FATHER (*pater*)/**HEAVEN** (*ouranos*) - Vine defines *pater* as "a nourisher, protector, upholder…" (p. 81) Vine defines *ouranos* as "to lift, to heaven… In the present life heaven is the region of the spiritual citizenship of believers, Phil. 3:20." (p. 208-209) This is the same word as used in Matthew 5:3 and 5:10 for "kingdom of heaven."

GIVE (*didomai*) – In Matthew 7:11, *didomai* is a third person singular future active indicative verb that means the fact of giving something at a future point in time.

GOOD GIFTS (*agathos*) – see definition of *agathos* in this verse above.

ASK HIM (*aiteo*) – In Matthew 7:11, *aiteo* is a third person plural present active indicative verb that means the fact of asking on an ongoing basis. For definition and description of *aiteo* see verse 7:7 above.

Barclay (*GOM*, Vol. 1) summarizes this passage by stating, "Jesus here lays down the twin facts that God will always answer our prayers in his way, in wisdom and in love; and that we must bring to God an undiscouraged [persistent] life of prayer, which tests the rightness of the things we pray for, and which tests our sincerity in asking for them." (p. 314)

7:12 **DO TO OTHERS** (*poieo*) – In Matthew 7:12, *poieo* is a third person plural present active imperative verb that means the command to do something to others on an ongoing basis.

SUMS UP (*eimi*) – In Matthew 7:12, *eimi* ("to be") is a third person singular present indicative verb that means that the fulfillment of the former phrase is the fulfillment of the Law and the Prophets.

Lloyd-Jones (*Sermon on the Mount*) summarizes Matthew 7:12 by stating, "The whole purpose and the real spirit behind it is this, that we are to love our neighbors as ourselves, that we are to love one another… That is the law and the prophets. It all comes down to that." (p. 210)

Application (A):

What insights about discipleship have you gained from this chapter?

While praying through this list of insights, ask God which of these you are already applying and which you need to start applying. Try to identify strengths and weaknesses, and prioritize which weaknesses God wants you to work on.

Identify the top priority issue that God wants you to work on and formulate a study/application plan to allow God to graciously begin his transforming work in your heart. What is God's top priority issue and how are you going to cooperate with him in this?

Is there a mentor or accountability partner who can help you by giving wise counsel, praying, encouraging, holding you accountable, etc.? Who is it and how/when will you contact him/her?

CHAPTER 19

Matthew 7:13-14 – Narrow Gate

^{7:13} **Enter ye in at the strait gate: for wide is the gate, and broad is the way, that leadeth to destruction, and many there be which go in thereat:** ¹⁴ **Because strait is the gate, and narrow is the way, which leadeth unto life, and few there be that find it.** (KJV)

Introduction (I): Go to biblegateway.com for additional translations and paraphrases.

(NIV) ^{7:13} "Enter through the narrow gate. For wide is the gate and broad is the road that leads to destruction, and many enter through it. ¹⁴ But small is the gate and narrow the road that leads to life, and only a few find it.

(NASB) ^{7:13} "Enter through the narrow gate; for the gate is wide and the way is broad that leads to destruction, and there are many who enter through it. ¹⁴ For the gate is small and the way is narrow that leads to life, and there are few who find it.

(Message) ^{7:13-14} "Don't look for shortcuts to God. The market is flooded with surefire, easygoing formulas for a successful life that can be practiced in your spare time. Don't fall for that stuff, even though crowds of people do. The way to life — to God! — is vigorous and requires total attention.

Discovery (D): Study Guide for Matthew 7:13-14 – Narrow Gate

Read the passage in the KJV and respond to the following questions:

1. (7:13-14) What does "enter ye in the strait [narrow] gate" mean and where does it lead?

2. (7:13-14) What does "wide [broad] is the way" mean and where does it lead?

3. (7:13-14) What are the characteristics and consequences of the "strait" and "wide" way of living? How does this relate to the Beatitudes and Salt and Light passages (Matthew 5:3-16)?

4. What is your interpretation and application of this passage?

Explanation (E):

7:13 **ENTER** (*eiserchomai*) – In Matthew 7:13, *eiserchomai* is a second person plural first aorist imperative verb that means the command to enter at a point in time. Vine (*Expository Dictionary of N.T. Words*) defines *eiserchomai* as "to come into (*eis*, in, *erchomai*, to come)..." (p. 34)

NARROW GATE (*stenochoreo*) – Vine defines *stehochoreo* as "to be pressed for room (*steno*, narrow, *choros*, a space)…" (p. 79)

WIDE (*platos*) – Vine defines *platos* as "connected with *plak*, a flat, broad surface, signifies to make broad…" (p. 154)

BROAD (*eurochoros*) – Vine defines *eurochoros* as "from *eurus*, broad, *chora*, a place, signifies, lit., (with) a broad place, i.e., broad, spacious, Matt. 7:13." (p. 154)

LEADS TO (*apago*) – In Matthew 7:13, *apago* is a nominative singular present active participle that means the ongoing action of leading to.

DESTRUCTION (*apoleia*) – Vine defines *apoleia* as "loss of well-being, not of being…" (p. 303)

MANY ENTER (*eiserchomai*) – In Matthew 7:13, *eiserchomai* is a nominative plural present participle that means ongoing entering into.

7:14 **SMALL** (*stenochoreo*)/**NARROW** (*thlibo*) – Vine defines *thlibo* as "to press, is translated 'narrow' in Matt. 7:14… i.e., hemmed in, like a mountain gorge…" (p. 101-102)

LEADS (*apago*) – In Matthew 7:14, *apago* is a nominative singular present active participle that means the ongoing action of leading to. See Matthew 7:13 for definition of *apago*.

LIFE (*zoe*) – Vine defines *zoe* as "that which is the common possession of all animals and men by nature…. of life as a principle." (p. 367)

FEW FIND IT (*heurisko*) – In Matthew 7:14, *heurisko* is a nominative plural present active participle that means the action of finding it. Vine defines *heurisko* as "(a) to find, either with previous search, e.g., Matt. 7:7, 8, or without, e.g., Matt. 27:32… (b) metaphorically, to find out by inquiry, or to learn, discover, e.g., Luke 19:48…" (p. 100)

Barclay (*GOM*, Vol. 1) states that, "We must always take one way or the other… (1) It is the difference between *the hard and the easy way*… (2) It is the difference between *the long and the short way*… (3) It is the difference between *the disciplined and the undisciplined way*… (4) It is the difference between *the thoughtful and unthoughtful way*… Everything in this world has two aspects – how it looks at the moment, and how it looks in the time to come. The easy way may look very inviting at the moment, and the hard way may look very daunting. The only way to get our values right is to see not the beginning but the end of the way, to see things not in the light of time but in the light of eternity." (p. 321-324)

Application (A):

What insights about discipleship have you gained from this chapter?

While praying through this list of insights, ask God which of these you are already applying and which you need to start applying. Try to identify strengths and weaknesses, and prioritize which weaknesses God wants you to work on.

Identify the top priority issue that God wants you to work on and formulate a study/application plan to allow God to graciously begin his transforming work in your heart. What is God's top priority issue and how are you going to cooperate with him in this?

Is there a mentor or accountability partner who can help you by giving wise counsel, praying, encouraging, holding you accountable, etc.? Who is it and how/when will you contact him/her?

CHAPTER 20

Matthew 7:15-23 – Fruit

7:15 Beware of false prophets, which come to you in sheep's clothing, but inwardly they are ravening wolves. 16 Ye shall know them by their fruits. Do men gather grapes of thorns, or figs of thistles? 17 Even so every good tree bringeth forth good fruit; but a corrupt tree bringeth forth evil fruit. 18 A good tree cannot bring forth evil fruit, neither can a corrupt tree bring forth good fruit. 19 Every tree that bringeth not forth good fruit is hewn down, and cast into the fire. 20 Wherefore by their fruits ye shall know them. 21 Not every one that saith unto me, Lord, Lord, shall enter into the kingdom of heaven; but he that doeth the will of my Father which is in heaven. 22 Many will say to me in that day, Lord, Lord, have we not prophesied in thy name? and in thy name have cast out devils? and in thy name done many wonderful works? 23 And then will I profess unto them, I never knew you: depart from me, ye that work iniquity. (KJV)

Introduction (I): Go to biblegateway.com for additional translations and paraphrases.

(NIV) 7:15 "Watch out for false prophets. They come to you in sheep's clothing, but inwardly they are ferocious wolves. 16 By their fruit you will recognize them. Do people pick grapes from thornbushes, or figs from thistles? 17 Likewise, every good tree bears good fruit, but a bad tree bears bad fruit. 18 A good tree cannot bear bad fruit, and a bad tree cannot bear good fruit. 19 Every tree that does not bear good fruit is cut down and thrown into the fire. 20 Thus, by their fruit you will recognize them. 21 "Not everyone who says to me, 'Lord, Lord,' will enter the kingdom of heaven, but only the one who does the will of my Father who is in heaven. 22 Many will say to me on that day, 'Lord, Lord, did we not prophesy in your name and in your name drive out demons and in your name perform many miracles?' 23 Then I will tell them plainly, 'I never knew you. Away from me, you evildoers!'

(NASB) ⁷:¹⁵ "Beware of the false prophets, who come to you in sheep's clothing, but inwardly are ravenous wolves. ¹⁶ You will know them by their fruits. Grapes are not gathered from thorn bushes nor figs from thistles, are they? ¹⁷ So every good tree bears good fruit, but the bad tree bears bad fruit. ¹⁸ A good tree cannot produce bad fruit, nor can a bad tree produce good fruit. ¹⁹ Every tree that does not bear good fruit is cut down and thrown into the fire. ²⁰ So then, you will know them by their fruits. ²¹ "Not everyone who says to Me, 'Lord, Lord,' will enter the kingdom of heaven, but he who does the will of My Father who is in heaven will enter. ²² Many will say to Me on that day, 'Lord, Lord, did we not prophesy in Your name, and in Your name cast out demons, and in Your name perform many miracles?' ²³ And then I will declare to them, 'I never knew you; DEPART FROM ME, YOU WHO PRACTICE LAWLESSNESS.'

(Message) ⁷:¹⁵⁻²⁰ "Be wary of false preachers who smile a lot, dripping with practiced sincerity. Chances are they are out to rip you off some way or other. Don't be impressed with charisma; look for character. Who preachers are is the main thing, not what they say. A genuine leader will never exploit your emotions or your pocketbook. These diseased trees with their bad apples are going to be chopped down and burned. ²¹⁻²³ "Knowing the correct password — saying 'Master, Master,' for instance — isn't going to get you anywhere with me. What is required is serious obedience—doing what my Father wills. I can see it now — at the Final Judgment thousands strutting up to me and saying, 'Master, we preached the Message, we bashed the demons, our God-sponsored projects had everyone talking.' And do you know what I am going to say? 'You missed the boat. All you did was use me to make yourselves important. You don't impress me one bit. You're out of here.'

Discovery (D): Study Guide for Matthew 7:15-23 – Fruit

Read the passage in the KJV and respond to the following questions:

1. (7:15) What does "Beware of false prophets" mean? What are the characteristics of false prophets and teachers? (see Jeremiah 23; Matthew 23; and I Corinthians 13)

2. (7:16-20) What does "Ye shall know them by their fruits" mean? What do the good and bad fruits look like? (see Galatians 5:19-26 and James 3:13-18)

3. (7:16-20) What are the results or consequences of producing good or bad fruit?

4. (7:21) What does "he that doeth the will of my Father" mean? (see I Thessalonians 4:3-8). How does this relate to the Beatitudes and Salt and Light passages (Matthew 5:3-16)?

5. (7:22-23) How is it possible to do such "wonderful works" in Jesus name and not know God? (See Hebrews 6:4-6)

6. What is your interpretation and application of this passage?

Explanation (E):

7:15 **WATCH OUT** (*prosecho*) – In Matthew 7:15, *prosecho* is a second person plural present imperative verb that means the command to keep watching out. Vine (*Expository Dictionary of the N.T.*) defines *prosecho* as "to hold to (*pros*, to, *echo*, to have, to hold), hence, to turn one's mind or attention to a thing by being on one's guard against it…" (p. 124)

FALSE PROPHETS (*pseudoprophetes*) – Vine defines *pseudoprophetes* as "a false prophet…" (p. 222) Kittle (*Theological Dictionary of the N.T.*) states that, "in the NT the word *pseudo-prophetes* covers various kinds of false prophets, e.g. Jewish prophets in Lk. 6:26; 2 Pet. 2:1, the magician in Acts 13:6, and false Christian teachers in 2 Pet.2:1; 2 Jn. 7; 1 Jn. 2:18 (cf. Jezebel in Rev. 2:20). False prophets are common in the last days (Mt. 24:11)… Prophets must be tested, not rationally, but spiritually and charismatically (1 Cor. 12:10) by other [mature leaders] (14:29). False prophets may perform miracles (Mk. 13:22; Rev. 13:13). Christological confession forms a test (1 Jn. 4:2-3). So do fruits (Mt. 7:16; cf. Rev. 2:20)." (p. 964)

COME (*erchomai*) – In Matthew 7:15, *erchomai* is a third person plural present indicative verb that means the fact of coming on an ongoing basis. Vine defines *erchomai* as "to come, or to go, signifies the act…" (p. 203)

GREEDY (*harpax*) – Vine defines *harpax* as "denotes pillage, plundering, robbery, extortion (akin to *harpazo*, to seize, carry off by force…)…" (p. 64)

7:16-20 **FRUIT** (*karpos*) – Vine defines *karpos* as "what is produced by the inherent energy of a living organism… metaphorically, (a) of works or deeds, fruit being the visible expression of power working inwardly and invisibly, the character of the fruit being evidence of the character of the power producing it, Matt. 7:16." (p. 133)

Barclay (*GOM*, Vol. 1) comments that, "This passage has much to say about evil fruits of the false prophets… (1) Teaching is false if it produces *a religion which consists solely or mainly in the observance of externals*… (2) Teaching is false if it produces *a religion which consists in prohibitions*… (3) Teaching is false if it produces *an easy religion*… (4) Teaching is false if it *divorces religion and life*… (5) Teaching is false if it produces *a religion which is arrogant and separatist*…" (p. 329-332)

7:21 **NOT EVERYONE WHO SAYS** (*lego*) – In Matthew 7:21, *lego* is a nominative singular present active participle that means speaking on an ongoing basis. Vine defines *lego* as "to pick out, gather, chiefly denotes to say, speak, affirm…" (p. 323)

LORD (*kurios*) – Vine defines *kurios* as "signifying having power (*kuros*) or authority… It is used (a) of an owner, as in Luke 19:33, cf. Matt. 20:8; Acts 16:16; Gal. 4:1; or of one who has the disposal of anything, as the Sabbath, Matt. 12:8; (b) of a master, i.e., one to whom service is due on any ground, Matt. 6:24; 24:50; Eph. 6:5; (c) of an Emperor or King, Acts 25:26; Rev. 17:14; (d) of idols, ironically, 1 Cor. 8:5, cf. Isa. 26:13; (e) as a title of respect addressed to a father, Matt. 21:30, a husband, 1 Pet. 3:6, a master, Matt. 13:27; Luke 13:8… (f) as a title of courtesy addressed to a stranger… (g) *kurios* is the Sept. and NT representative of Heb. Jehovah ('Lord" in Eng. Versions)…" (p. 379)"

WILL ENTER (*eiserchomai*) – In Matthew 7:21, *eiserchomai* is a third person singular future indicative verb that means the fact of entering in the future.

KINGDOM (*basileia*)/**HEAVEN** (*ouranos*) - Vine points out that *basileia* means "the sovereignty and dominion of God and/or the territory or people over whom God rules." (p. 294) Vine defines *ouranos* as "to lift, to heave… In the present life heaven is the region of the spiritual citizenship of believers, Phil. 3:20." (p. 208-209) This is the same word as used in Matthew 5:3 and 5:10 for "kingdom of heaven."

HE WHO DOES (*poieo*) – In Matthew 7:21, *poieo* is a nominative singular present active participle that means the act of doing on an ongoing basis. Vine defines *poieo* as "to do, i.e., to adopt a way of expressing by act the thoughts and feelings." (p. 330)

THE WILL (*thelema*) – Vine defines *thelema* as "(a) objectively, that which is willed, of the will of God, e.g., Matt. 18:14… the fulfilling being a sign of spiritual relationships to the Lord; John 4:34…" (p. 216)

FATHER (*pater*)/**HEAVEN** (*ouranos*) – for definitions and descriptions of *pater* and *ouranos* see Matthew 7:11.

7:22 **PROPHECY** (*propheteuo*) – In Matthew 7:22, *propheteuo* is a first person plural first aorist indicative verb that means the fact of prophecy at a point in time. Vine defines *propheteuo* as "telling forth the Divine counsels, e.g., Matt. 7:22…" (p. 222) Kittle states that, "In the NT *prophetes* is easily the most common term of the group [of words relating to prophecy]. It occurs 144 times, mostly in Matthew, Luke, Acts, and John. The prophet is normally a biblical proclaimer of a divine inspired message… The biblical prophet can predict the future (cf. Acts 11:28), can know the past (Jn. 4:19), and can look into the heart (Lk. 7:39), but is essentially a proclaimer of the word…" (p. 960)

DRIVE OUT (*ekballo*) – In Matthew 7:22, *ekballo* is a first person plural second aorist indicative verb that means the fact of casting out demons at a point in time.

DEMONS (*diamonion*) – Vine defines *diamonion* as "the neuter of the adjective *diamonios*, pertaining to a demon… Demons are the spiritual agents acting in all idolatry." (p. 291) Kittle describes *diamonion* as, "In the main the NT follows the OT. There is no reference to the spirits of the dead. *Diamon*, which suggests a divine intermediary, is avoided. Angels and demons are basically antithetical. There are few references to demons except in the case of demon possession… Because of faith in God, the fear of demons is expelled… " (p. 139)

MIRACLES (*dunamis*) – Vine defines *dunamis* as "power, inherent ability, is used of works of a supernatural origin and character, such as could not be produced by natural agents or means." (p. 75) *Dunamis* is the object of *poieo* ("to do") that is a first person plural first aorist active indicative verb.

7:23 **I WILL TELL THEM** (*homologeo*) – in Matthew 7:23, *homologeo* is a first person singular future active indicative verb that means the fact of telling in the future.

DEPART (*apochoreo*) – In Matthew 7:23, *apochoreo* is a second person plural present imperative verb that means the command to depart from on an ongoing basis. Vine describes *apochoreo* as "lit., 'to come or go away' (*apo*), hence, 'to set off, depart'…" (p. 159)

NEVER KNEW YOU (*ginosko*) – In Matthew 7:23, *ginosko* is a first person singular second aorist active indicative verb that means the fact of never knowing at a point in time.

EVIL DOERS (*anomia*) – Vine defines *anomia* as "lawlessness (*a*, negative, *nomos*, law), is used in a way which indicates the meaning of being lawlessness or wickedness." (p. 260)

Barclay (*GOM*, Vol. 1) states that, "There are two great permanent truths in this passage. There is only one way in which people's sincerity can be proved, and that is by their practice. Fine words can never be a substitute for fine deeds. There is only one proof of love, and that proof is obedience… Faith without practice is a contradiction in terms, and love without obedience is an impossibility… All through [this passage] runs the certainty that the day of reckoning comes. Some people may succeed over a period in maintaining the pretenses and the disguises, but there comes a day when the pretenses are shown for what they are, and the disguises are stripped away. We may deceive others with our words, but we cannot deceive God." (p. 334)

Lloyd-Jones (*Sermon on the Mount*) comments that, "You may have to wait before you can see any true evidence. God sees it from the beginning, but we are very slow to see these things. But what a man is, he is bound to show. He will show it in his teaching for certain, he will show it in his life also. It is quite inevitable. We can say, therefore, that true Christian belief must of necessity produce that characteristic type of living… A man's final belief is bound to manifest itself, sooner or later, in his life." (p. 255)

Application (A):

What insights about discipleship have you gained from this chapter?

While praying through this list of insights, ask God which of these you are already applying and which you need to start applying. Try to identify strengths and weaknesses, and prioritize which weaknesses God wants you to work on.

Identify the top priority issue that God wants you to work on and formulate a study/application plan to allow God to graciously begin his transforming work in your heart. What is God's top priority issue and how are you going to cooperate with him in this?

Is there a mentor or accountability partner who can help you by giving wise counsel, praying, encouraging, holding you accountable, etc.? Who is it and how/when will you contact him/her?

CHAPTER 21

Matthew 7:24-27 – Builders

^{7:24} Therefore whosoever heareth these sayings of mine, and doeth them, I will liken him unto a wise man, which built his house upon a rock: ²⁵ And the rain descended, and the floods came, and the winds blew, and beat upon that house; and it fell not: for it was founded upon a rock. ²⁶ And every one that heareth these sayings of mine, and doeth them not, shall be likened unto a foolish man, which built his house upon the sand: ²⁷ And the rain descended, and the floods came, and the winds blew, and beat upon that house; and it fell: and great was the fall of it. (KJV)

Introduction (I):   Go to biblegateway.com for additional translations and paraphrases.

(NIV) ^{7:24} "Therefore everyone who hears these words of mine and puts them into practice is like a wise man who built his house on the rock. ²⁵ The rain came down, the streams rose, and the winds blew and beat against that house; yet it did not fall, because it had its foundation on the rock. ²⁶ But everyone who hears these words of mine and does not put them into practice is like a foolish man who built his house on sand. ²⁷ The rain came down, the streams rose, and the winds blew and beat against that house, and it fell with a great crash.

(NASB) ^{7:24} "Therefore everyone who hears these words of Mine and acts on them, may be compared to a wise man who built his house on the rock. ²⁵ And the rain fell, and the floods came, and the winds blew and slammed against that house; and yet it did not fall, for it had been founded on the rock. ²⁶ Everyone who hears these words of Mine and does not act on them, will be like a foolish man who built his house on the sand. ²⁷ The rain fell, and the floods came, and the winds blew and slammed against that house; and it fell — and great was its fall."

(Message) [7:24-25] "These words I speak to you are not incidental additions to your life, homeowner improvements to your standard of living. They are foundational words, words to build a life on. If you work these words into your life, you are like a smart carpenter who built his house on solid rock. Rain poured down, the river flooded, a tornado hit — but nothing moved that house. It was fixed to the rock. [26-27] "But if you just use my words in Bible studies and don't work them into your life, you are like a stupid carpenter who built his house on the sandy beach. When a storm rolled in and the waves came up, it collapsed like a house of cards."

Discovery (D): Study Guide for Matthew 7:24-27 – Builders

Read the passage in the KJV and respond to the following questions:

1. (7:24) What does it mean to be a "wise man" who "built his house upon the rock"? Why is "hearing" and "doing" important?

2. (7:26) What does it mean to be a "foolish man" who "built his house upon the sand"? Why does this builder hear but not do? (See The Parable of the Sower - Matthew 13:1-23)

3. (7:25, 27) What happens to the houses that the wise and foolish builders built when "the rain descended, and the floods came, and the winds blew, and beat upon that house"?

4. (7:24, 26) What is the importance of foundations and how do we develop a foundation of rock? (see I Timothy 1:5)

5. (7:24-27) What is your interpretation and application of this passage?

Explanation (E):

7:24 **HEARS** (*akouo*) – In Matthew 7:24, *akouo* is a third person singular present active indicative verb that means the fact of hearing on an ongoing basis. Vine (*Expository Dictionary of the N.T.*) defines *akouo* as "(a) a sense of hearing… (b) the organ of hearing… (c) a thing heard… (d) the receiving of a message…" (p. 205-206)

WORDS (*logos*) – Vine defines *logos* as "the expression of thought – not the mere name of an object." (p. 229)

PUTS THEM INTO PRACTICE (*poieo*) – In Matthew 7:24, *poieo* is a third person singular present active indicative verb that means the fact of doing on an ongoing basis. Vine defines *poieo* as "to adopt a way of expressing by act the thoughts and feelings." (p. 330)

IS LIKE (*homoioo*) – In Matthew 7:24, *homoioo* is a third person singular future passive indicative verb that means the fact of being likened upon in the future.

WISE MAN (*phronimos*) - Vine defines *phronimos* as "prudent, sensible, practically wise, Matt. 7:24…" (p. 222)

Barclay (*GOM*, Vol. 1) comments that, "Knowledge only becomes relevant when it is translated into action… Knowledge must become action; theory must become practice; theology must become life." (p. 336)

BUILT (*oikodomeo*)/**HOUSE** (*oikos*) – In Matthew 7:24, *oikodomeo* is a third person singular first aorist active indicative verb that means the fact of building at a point in time. Vine defines *oikodomeo* as "to build a house (*oikos*, house, *domeo*, to build), hence, to build anything, e.g., Matt. 7:24…" (p. 156)

ROCK (*petra*) – Vine defines *petra* as "a mass of rock, as distinct from *petros*, a detached stone or boulder, or a stone that might be thrown or easily moved." (p. 302)

7:25 **RAIN CAME DOWN** (*katabaino*) – In Matthew 7:25, *katabaino* is a third person singular aorist indicative verb that means the fact of rain coming down or descending at a point in time. Vine defines *katabaino* as "to go down (*kata*, down, *baino*, to go), used for various kinds of motion on the ground (e.g., going, walking, stepping), is usually translated to descend." (p. 296)

STREAMS ROSE (*erchomai*) – In Matthew 7:25, *erchomai* is first person singular second aorist indicative verb that means the fact of flooding at a point in time.

WINDS BLEW (*pneo*) – In Matthew 7:25, *pneo* is a third person plural first aorist indicative verb that means the fact of the wind blowing at a point in time.

BEAT AGAINST (*proskopto*) – In Matthew 7:25, *prokopto* is a third person plural fist aorist indicative verb that means the fact of the wind having beaten against the house at a point in time. Vine defines *prokopto* as "'to stumble, to strike against' (*pros*, 'to or against,' *kopto*, 'to strike'), is once used of a storm 'beating' upon a house, Matt. 7:27." (p. 54)

DID NOT FALL (*pipto*) – In Matthew 7:25, *pipto* is a third person singular second aorist indicative verb that means the fact of not falling down at a point in time. Vine defines *pipto* as "of things, falling into ruin, or failing, e.g., Matt. 7:25…" (p. 73)

BECAUSE IT HAD ITS FOUNDATION (*themelioo*)/**ROCK** (*petra*) – In Matthew 7:25, *themelioo* is a third person singular perfect passive verb that means to have been built on or founded on. Vine defines *themelioo* as "to lay a foundation, to found…" (p. 128) For definition of *petra* see verse 7:24 above.

7:26-27 - Matthew 7:26-27 is similar to 7:24-25 in word and tense construction with the exception of the contrast between doing/not doing and wise/foolish.

DOES NOT PUT THEM INTO PRACTICE (*poieo*) – In Matthew 7:26, *poieo* is a nominative singular present active participle that means ongoing failure to put what one is hearing into practice. Also, *akouo* ("to hear") is a present active participle. Both participles are connected to the main verb *homoioo* ("to be like").

FOOLISH (*moros*) – Vine defines *moros* as "dull, sluggish (from the root *muh*, to be silly); hence, stupid, foolish… *moros* scorns the heart and character…" (p. 114)

SAND (*ammos*) – Vine defines *ammos* as "sand or sandy ground…an insecure foundation, Matthew 7:26…" (p. 319)

GREAT (*mega*)/**CRASH** (*ptosis*) – Vine defines *ptosis* as "of the overthrow of a building, Matthew 7:27…" (p. 73)

Lloyd-Jones (*Sermon on the Mount*) comments that, "The best approach to this particular picture is to look at it as the third in a series. The first, in verses 15-20, concerning the false prophet, was designed to warn us against the danger of being deceived by appearances… The second picture [verses 7:21-23] is one of people who assume that everyone who says 'Lord, Lord' shall enter the kingdom of heaven. This is a picture designed to warn us against the danger of deceiving ourselves in terms of what we believe, or in terms of our zeal and fervor, and our own activities… We are now going to look at the third and last picture. I suggest at once, in order to concentrate attention, that our Lord's chief concern in this picture is to warn us against the danger of seeking and desiring only the benefits and blessings of salvation, and resting upon our apparent possession of them." (p. 294-295)

Application (A):

What insights about discipleship have you gained from this chapter?

While praying through this list of insights, ask God which of these you are already applying and which you need to start applying. Try to identify strengths and weaknesses, and prioritize which weaknesses God wants you to work on.

Identify the top priority issue that God wants you to work on and formulate a study/application plan to allow God to graciously begin his transforming work in your heart. What is God's top priority issue and how are you going to cooperate with him in this?

Is there a mentor or accountability partner who can help you by giving wise counsel, praying, encouraging, holding you accountable, etc.? Who is it and how/when will you contact him/her?

CHAPTER 22

Matthew 7:28-29 – Conclusion

7:28 **And it came to pass, when Jesus had ended these sayings, the people were astonished at his doctrine:** **29** **For he taught them as one having authority, and not as the scribes.** (KJV)

Introduction (I): Go to biblegateway.com for additional translations and paraphrases.

(NIV) 7:28 When Jesus had finished saying these things, the crowds were amazed at his teaching, 29 because he taught as one who had authority, and not as their teachers of the law."

(NASB) 7:28 When Jesus had finished these words, the crowds were amazed at His teaching; 29 for He was teaching them as one having authority, and not as their scribes.

(Message) 7:28-29 When Jesus concluded his address, the crowd burst into applause. They had never heard teaching like this. It was apparent that he was living everything he was saying — quite a contrast to their religion teachers! This was the best teaching they had ever heard.

Discovery (D): **Study Guide for Matthew 7:28-29 – Conclusion**

Read the passage in the KJV and respond to the following questions:

1. (7:28) Who heard Jesus' teaching and were "amazed"? (Contrast this with Matthew 5:1-2) What do you think happened?

2. (7:28) Why was the crowd "amazed"?

3. (7:29) What does "authority" mean? (See Matthew 28:18 and Acts 1:7-8) How does this "authority" set Jesus' teaching apart from the Teachers of the law?

4. (7:28-29) How does this "amazing… authority" relate to the Beatitudes and Salt and Light in Matthew 5:3-16?

5. (8:1-4) What happened after Jesus finished teaching?

6. (7:28-29) What is your interpretation and application of this passage?

Explanation (E):

7:28 WHEN JESUS HAD FINISHED (*teleo*)/**WORDS** (*logos*) – In Matthew 7:28, *teleo* is a third person singular active indicative verb that means the fact of having finished at a point in time. Vine (*Expository Dictionary of the N.T.*) defines *teleo* as "to bring to an end (*telos*, an end)…" (p. 101)

THE CROWDS WERE AMAZED (*ekplesso*) – In Matthew 7:28, *ekplesso* is a third person plural imperfect passive verb that means "continued action in past time…" (Machen, *N.T. Greek*, p. 65) Vine defines *ekplesso* as "from *ek*, out of, *plesso*, to strike, lit., to strike out, signifies to be exceedingly struck in mind, to be astonished…" (p. 52)

TEACHING (*didasko*) – Vine defines *didasko* as "to give instruction…" (p. 111) Kittle (*Theological Dictionary of the N.T.*) states that, "Of the 95 instances [used in the N.T.], almost two thirds are in the Gospels and Acts (and only ten in Paul)… [1.] *didaskein* is one of the main functions of Jesus (Mt. 4:23; 9:35; 11:1). He teaches in the synagogues (Mt. 9:35) and the temple (Mk. 12:35) as well as outside. [2.] The form of his teaching is that of a typical teacher of the age. At Nazareth he reads Scripture, seats himself, and expounds the passage (Lk. 4-16ff.). He also sits to teach in Mt. 5:1ff; Mk. 9:35; Lk. 5:3. [3.] The material of Jesus is also traditional. He starts from Scripture in Lk. 4:16ff.; Mt. 5:21ff. Yet he does not stop at the law and opposes casuistic exposition. He aims to order all life in relation to God and neighbor (Mt. 22:37ff.), appeals to the will, and calls for decisions for or against God. Like the rabbis, he finds a revelation of God's will in Scripture (Mt. 5:17-18). The main difference lies in his own self-awareness as the Son. It is in virtue of his person that his teaching causes astonishment (Mk. 1:22; Mt. 7:28-29).., [4.] The novel feature in the Gospels is the absence of the intellectual emphasis which is common everywhere else among the Greek writers… and which develops in rabbinic exegesis in an effort to check the disintegrating force of Hellenism…" (p. 162)

7:29 BECAUSE HE TAUGHT (*didasko*) – In Matthew 7:29, *didasko* is a nominative singular present active participle that means teaching on an ongoing basis.

AUTHORITY (*exousia*) – Vine defines *exousia* as "authority (from impersonal verb *exesti*, 'it is lawful'). From the meaning of leave or permission, or liberty of doing as one pleases, it passed to that of the ability or strength with which one is endued, then to that of the power of authority, the right to exercise power, e.g., Matt. 9:6… or the power of rule or government, the power of one whose will and command must be obeyed by others, e.g., Matt. 28:8…" (p. 89) *Exousia* is the object of the present participle ("to be").

TEACHERS OF THE LAW (*grammateus*) – Vine defines *grammateus* as "from *gramma*, a writing, denotes a scribe, a man of letters, a teacher of the law… Their function regarding the law were to teach it, to develop it, and use it in connection with the Sanhedrin and various local courts…" (p. 328)

Lloyd-Jones (*Sermon on the Mount*) comments that, "These two verses are by no means an idle or useless kind of epilogue. They are of great importance… There are two main reasons for saying that. The first is that, ultimately, the authority of the sermon derives from the Preacher… [The second,] I imagine, however, that what really astonished these people over and above His general authority was what He said, and in particular what He said about Himself. That, most surely, must have amazed them." (p. 327, 330)

NOTE: It is important to note that immediately after Jesus finished the Sermon on the Mount, He healed a man with leprosy (8:1-4). Again, we see that Jesus' words and deeds of compassion are inseparable.

Application (A):

What insights about discipleship have you gained from this chapter?

While praying through this list of insights, ask God which of these you are already applying and which you need to start applying. Try to identify strengths and weaknesses, and prioritize which weaknesses God wants you to work on.

Identify the top priority issue that God wants you to work on and formulate a study/application plan to allow God to graciously begin his transforming work in your heart. What is God's top priority issue and how are you going to cooperate with him in this?

Is there a mentor or accountability partner who can help you by giving wise counsel, praying, encouraging, holding you accountable, etc.? Who is it and how/when will you contact him/her?

Appendix A

The Presence of the Future

(Adapted from George Eldon Ladd, *The Presence of the Future*
and *The Gospel of the Kingdom*;
John Wimber, *Power Evangelism*;
and Kevin Springer (editor), *The Kingdom and the Power*,
chapter 7: The Empowered Christian Life by James I. Packer)

"The presence of the Kingdom of God was seen as God's dynamic reign invading the present age without transforming it into the age to come" (*The Presence of the Future*, p. 149).

"Our Gospel is a Gospel of glorious promise and hope. Yes, the best, the glorious best, is yet to be. And yet we are not to live alone for the future. The future has already begun. The Age to Come has reached into This Age; the Kingdom of God has come unto you. The eternal life which belongs to tomorrow is here today. The fellowship which we shall know when we see him face to face is already ours, in part but in reality. The transforming life of the Spirit of God which will one day transform our bodies has come to indwell us and to transform our characters and personalities" (*The Gospel of the Kingdom*, p. 78).

"Many Christians [in the West] either exclude the supernatural from their worldview or consign it to the transcendent tier, where it can have no effect in their lives; by doing so they exclude God's power from their theology and its practice. Resisting what they cannot fully control or always understand, they miss out on doing Christ's work today" (*Power Evangelism*, p. 81).

The Excluded Middle (*Power Evangelism*, chapter 5: Signs and Wonders and Worldviews):

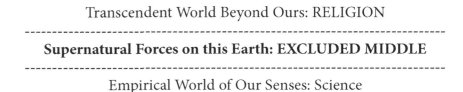

Transcendent World Beyond Ours: RELIGION

Supernatural Forces on this Earth: EXCLUDED MIDDLE

Empirical World of Our Senses: Science

"Instead of being forced to the extremes of empiricism or animism, Christians see the possibility though not the necessity for supernatural intervention in all earthly experience" (*Power Evangelism*, p. 81).

"It is clear from the New Testament that God meant His power to accompany the gospel, and to find expression through its messengers and in the lives of those to whom the message comes" (*The Kingdom and the Power*, p. 211).

1. "First, in the Gospels, we encounter works of power in the physical realm, including miracles of nature and healings of all sorts…

2. "Second, one reads on in the New Testament and finds that words of power in Christian communication are very much a part of the gospel story and of the story of the new church…

3. "Third, the New Testament speaks not only of God's power in the miraculous and in the communication of the gospel, but also of God's power at work in us, enabling us to understand and to do what we otherwise could not do" (chapter 7: The Empowered Christian Life by J.I. Packer).

"This leads me to five theses about the manifestation of God's power among His people today…

1. "It is right to bring the supernatural into prominence and to raise Christians' expectations with regard to it…

2. "It is right to aspire to use one's God-given gifts in powerful and useful ministry…

3. "It is right to want to be a channel of divine power into other people's lives at their point of need…

4. "It is right to want to see God's power manifest in a way that has significant evangelistic effect…

5. "It is right to want to be divinely empowered for righteousness, for moral victories, for deliverance from bad habits, and for pleasing God" (chapter 7: The Empowered Christian Life by J.I. Packer).

Outline of Bible-Centered Leadership

(compiled from J. Robert Clinton's
Having a Ministry that Lasts: Becoming a Bible-Centered Leader)

The Endangered Species of "Bible-Centered Leaders"
- There is a desperate need for Bible-Centered leaders
- We can become one
- This course is designed to help us become one

Biblical References (Clinton's translation):
- **Isaiah 40: 8 - A Lasting Source**
"The grass withers, the flower fades; but the Word of our God will stand forever."

- **II Timothy 3: 16-17 - A Guarantee About the Source**
"Every Scripture inspired of God is profitable for teaching, for setting things right, for confronting, for inspiring righteous living, in order that God's leader be thoroughly equipped to lead God's people."

- **II Timothy 2: 15 – The Proper Response to the Guarantee**
"Make every effort to be pleasing to God, a Bible-Centered leader who is completely confident in using God's Word with impact in lives."

Effective leaders should have an appropriate, unique, lifelong plan for mastering the Word in order to use it with impact in their ministries.

The Notion of Core:
1. All leaders have at least one word gift; most have a set of word gifts.
2. There are three different levels of word gifts: Foundational, Secondary, and Remote.
3. Each level requires a different kind of mastery of the Word.
4. All leaders have core items [books and passages] in the Bible that are important to them.

Life-long Bible Mastery Paradigm:
- It is individualized
- It builds on strength
- It is doable

- It is a process
- It focuses on using the Bible with impact
- It is reproducible

A Bible-Centered Leader refers to a leader whose leadership is informed by the Bible, who has been personally shaped by Biblical values, [and who] has grasped the intent of Scriptural books and their content in such a way as to apply them to current situations and who uses the Bible in ministry so as to impact followers (Clinton).

OT Examples of Bible-Centered Leaders:
- *Joshua* – "Courageous Leader"
- *David* – "Worship Leader"
- *Jeremiah* – "Catalytic Leader"
- *Daniel* – "Stabilizing Leader"
- *Ezra* – "Impact Leader"

NT Examples of Bible-Centered Leaders:
- *Jesus* – "Authoritative Leader"
- *Peter* – "Evangelistic Leader"
- *Paul* – "Pioneering Leader"

Introduction to Core and Word Gifts - Leaders usually have favorite Bible books, or special passages, which God has used mightily in their own lives to spur their growth or solve their problems or otherwise meet them. It is these books or special passages which form the basis for much of what they share with others in their ministries.

Core Items include:
- *Core Set* – "a collection of very important Bible books, usually from 5-20, which are or have been extremely meaningful…"

- *Core Selection* – "[a collection of] important passages, key biographical characters, special Psalms, special parables, special values or key topics which are or have been extremely meaningful…"

1. Persons who are gifted with the teaching gift in combination with other Word Gifts will usually have a larger core set (10-20). Persons who are gifted with other Word Gifts but not the teaching gift will have smaller core sets (5-10). One can expect core items to expand over time. But the major portion of core items will be discovered in the first 10-15 years of ministry.

2. Over a lifetime, a person should be challenged to master his/her core set and to have good familiarity with the rest of the Bible. This is a doable goal. It is one that will result in productive ministry.

3. Individuals will have a range of core items to be mastered over a lifetime.

Range *"refers to the extent of one's core items and includes the size and kind of core items."*

4. You can expect your range to grow over time until you reach your capacity and level of gifting.

5. Build a base on which you can advance.

Three (3) Levels of *Word Gifting*:

Foundational Word Gifts – "the major thrust of these gifts is the explanation of God and God's will" (Clinton).

- Teaching
- Exhortation
- Prophecy

Secondary Word Gifts – "their major function is… using God's word to accomplish… major tasks in the body of Christ" (Clinton).

- Apostleship
- Evangelism
- Pastor
- Leadership

Remote Word Gifts – "the operation of these gifts [involves] the primary dependency… on the Holy Spirit and not an accumulated body of knowledge" (Clinton).

- Word of wisdom
- Word of knowledge
- Word of faith
- Discernment

The "Equipping Formula":

Component 1: **Devotional Input** (Ongoing)
Component 2: **Mastery** (Ongoing)
Component 3: **Familiarity Reading** (Situational)
Component 4: **Situational Study** (of specific Books and/or passages to meet personal and/or ministry needs)

Component 1: Devotional Input (from any Core Item)

Devotional Input – "regular devotional input means a disciplined quiet time in which you use the Word to feed your soul and to grow in your intimacy with God and His ways."

1. Make sure you have a right heart attitude;
2. Let God speak to you;
3. Talk to God prayerfully during your quiet time; and
4. Share with others what happens in your quiet time.

Component 2: Mastery (of Core Items)

Core Work "refers to the yearly on-going study of one or more of your core items,

1. with a view of advancing your knowledge of the core item(s), and
2. to design communication events to use the results of those studies" (Clinton).

Core work can involve:
- Study of core books,
- Study of core passages, Psalms, and/or parables,
- Study of core biographical material,
- Study of core values, and/or
- Study of core topics.

Component 3: Familiarity Reading (of weak Bible portions)

Familiarity Reading "refers to a leader's reading of Scripture so as to stimulate remembrance of it and to provide an opportunity for discovery of new Core materials" (Clinton).

Component 4: Situational Study (of specific Books and/or passages to meet personal and/or ministry needs)

> **Situational Study** "refers to the special study that a leader does in the Bible which arises due to needs in a given situation or to ministry needs in general" (Clinton).

Appendix C

Canonization
How Did We Get the Bible?

(adapted from *The Canon of Scripture* by F. F. Bruce)

Process of Canonization:

A. **Old Testament**
1. Law was canonized first (early in the period after the return from the Babylonian exile – see Nehemiah 8:1-9, 38)
2. Prophets were canonized next (late in the third century BC – see Jeremiah 7:25, Ezekiel 38:17, Zechariah 1:4, 7:7 and Daniel 9:2)
3. Writings were last (end of the first century AD at Council of Jamnia in 70 AD)
4. Greek Old Testament (Septuagint) – earliest references between 250-150 BC (used by Greek-speaking Jews) – included Hebrew Bible and some non-canonical materials (53 total books)
5. Dead Sea Scrolls (found in 1947 at Qumran near the Dead Sea) – about 500 documents which were written during the two centuries prior to 70 AD (100 of these documents being copies of books of the Hebrew Bible – copies of all books except Esther)

B. **New Testament**
1. Early Church – Marcion (140 AD) listed 11 NT books (Luke and 10 Pauline letters) as accepted early Christian documents. Irenaeus (130-202 AD) listed the 4 Gospels, 13 Pauline letters, 3 non-Pauline letters and Revelation as accepted Christian documents.
2. Old Latin version (150-170 AD) included the 4 Gospels, 13 Pauline letters, 4 non-Pauline letters and Revelation.
3. 4th Century – Eusebius of Caesarea (325-340 AD) differentiated accepted, disputed, rejected and heretical books. His list included 4 Gospels, 13 Pauline letters, Hebrews, I Peter, I John and Revelation as accepted (James, II Peter, II & III John and Jude were disputed). Athanasius (367 AD) was first to list all 27 NT books as accepted.
4. Third Council of Carthage (397 AD) – Western church officially accepted 27 books as "canonical" books.

5. Latin Vulgate (404 AD) – official Roman Catholic Bible (designated at Council of Trent in 1546 AD) authored by Jerome established order of NT books.

6. Early Manuscripts – John Ryland manuscript, 130 AD, Chester Beaty papyri, 155 AD, and Bodmer papyri, 200 AD.

Criteria for Canonization:

A. **Old Testament**
   1. Acceptance in the Jewish community
   2. Acceptance by Christ
   3. Acceptance by the Apostles

B. **New Testament**
   1. Apostolic authority – written by an Apostle or someone closely associated with an Apostle
   2. Antiquity – written during the Apostolic age
   3. Orthodoxy – teaching consistent with Apostolic faith
   4. Catholicity – accepted by the wider church
   5. Tradition – accepted by wider church over the years
   6. Inspiration – recognized by wider church as having been inspired by the Holy Spirit

Appendix D
Reliability of the Bible
Is the Bible Reliable?

(adapted from *He Walked Among Us* by Josh McDowell and Bill Wilson)

I. **Critical Issues of Authenticity:**
   A. Are the books of the Bible historically credible?
   B. Did Jesus actually live?
   C. Was Jesus who the Bible claims him to be?

II. **Did Jesus Actually Live?**
   A. Biblical evidence
      1. Bibliographical test – over 22,000 copies of NT manuscripts in existence today (more manuscript authority than any other literature from antiquity)
      2. Internal evidence test – written by eyewitnesses (i.e. Luke 1:1-3, 3:1; John 19:35, II Peter 1:16; I John 1:3)

   B. External evidence
      1. Ancient secular writers – Thallus' (52 AD) and Phlegon's (140 AD) references to the crucifixion are quoted by Julius Africanus in his historical writings (221 AD)
      2. Josephus – 3 passages in his Antiquities (completed in 93 AD): chronology, John the Baptist, James and Jesus
      3. Early church fathers – Eusebius (130 AD) makes reference to NT authors and their writings (John, Mark, and Peter) and Irenaeus (180 AD) makes reference to NT authors and their writings (Matthew, Peter, Paul, Mark, Luke, and John)

III. **Was Jesus Who the Bible Claims Him to Be?**
   A. Prophetic evidence
      1. Fulfilled OT Messianic prophecies (322 prophetic predictions literally fulfilled)
      2. Jesus claimed to be the Messiah (79 of 80 "son of man" references in NT refer to Jesus, also see Luke 4:14-29)

   B. Empty tomb

C. Apostolic evidence
1. Eyewitness accounts (Luke 24:48; John 15:27; Acts 1:8, 2:24, 2:32, 3:15, 4:33, 5:32, 10:39, 10:41, 13:31, 22:15, 23:11, 26:16; I Corinthians 15:4-9, 15:15; I John 1:2)
2. Convinced of his life, death and resurrection (Luke 1:1-4)
3. Died for their beliefs (Peter, Andrew, Philip, Simon, James, son of Alphaeus, Bartholomew – crucified; Matthew and James, son of Zebedee – sword; Thaddaeus – arrows; James, brother of Jesus – stoned; Thomas – spear; John – natural causes

D. Evidence demands a verdict – Jesus was either:
1. A liar
2. Crazy
3. Who he claimed to be

Appendix E
Inductive Bible Study Methodology
Principles of Interpretation and Application

(adapted from *Studying, Interpreting, and Applying the Bible*
by Walter Hendrichsen and Gayle Jackson)

Review of Inductive Bible Study Method:
I. **Assumptions:**
    1. The Bible is authoritative
    2. The Bible contains its own laws of interpretation
    3. The primary aim of interpretation is to discover the author's meaning
    4. Language can communicate spiritual truth

II. **Review of four basic parts in studying the Bible correctly:**
    1. Observation – "What do I see?"
    2. Interpretation – "What does it mean?"
    3. Correlation – "How does this relate to what the rest of the Bible says?"
    4. Application – "What does it mean to me?"

Principles of Interpretation:
I. **General principles:**
    1. Work from the assumption that the Bible is authoritative
    2. The Bible interprets itself; Scripture best explains Scripture
    3. Saving faith and the Holy Spirit are necessary for us to understand and properly interpret the Scriptures
    4. Interpret personal experience in the light of Scripture and not Scripture in light of personal experience
    5. Biblical examples are authoritative only when supported by a command
    6. The primary purpose of the Bible is to change our lives, not increase our knowledge
    7. Each Christian has the right and responsibility to investigate and interpret the Word of God for himself
    8. Church history is important but not decisive in the interpretation of Scripture
    9. The promises of God contained throughout the Bible are available through the Holy Spirit for the believers of every generation

II. **Grammatical principles:**
1. Scripture has only one meaning and should be understood as true and applicable
2. Interpret words in harmony with their meaning in the times of the author
3. Interpret a word in relation to its sentence and context
4. Interpret a passage in harmony with its context
5. When an inanimate object is used to describe a living being, the statement may be considered figurative
6. When an expression is out of character with the thing described, the statement may be considered figurative
7. The principle parts and figures of a parable represent certain realities. Consider only these principal parts and figures when drawing conclusions
8. Interpret the words of the prophets in their usual, literal and historical sense, unless the context or manner in which they are fulfilled clearly indicates they have a symbolic meaning. Their fulfillment may be in installments, each fulfillment being a pledge of that which is to follow

III. **Historical principles:**
1. Since Scripture originated in a historical context, it can be understood only in the light of Biblical history
2. Though God's revelation in the Scripture is progressive, both Old and New Testaments are essential parts of this revelation and form a unit
3. Historical facts or events become symbols of spiritual truths only if the Scriptures so designate them

IV. **Theological principles:**
1. You must understand the Bible grammatically before you can understand it theologically
2. A doctrine cannot be considered biblical unless it sums up and includes all that the Scriptures say about it
3. When two doctrines taught in the Bible appear to be contradictory, accept both as scriptural in the confident belief they will resolve themselves into a higher unity
4. A teaching merely implied in Scripture may be considered biblical when a comparison of related passages supports it

Principles of Application

I. **Foundational Principles:**
1. Application must be focused on pleasing God rather than pleasing others

2. Every problem a person has is related to his or her concept of God
3. Attitude is as important as action in obeying God's commands
4. Surrender is the cornerstone of all application. Refusal to surrender blurs our ability to discover and do God's will
5. Application is a process, not a single event

II. Principles of Personal Responsibility:
1. In those areas of life not addressed by the Scriptures, we must develop personal convictions to govern our behavior
2. When applying the Scriptures, we must made a distinction between the positive and negative commandments
3. Each person is individually responsible for applying the Scriptures to his or her own life
4. In all things, we must be teachable. We must be willing to admit that we are wrong, change direction, and appear inconsistent
5. The acknowledgement of wrong must be followed by restitution when it is within our power

III. Principles of Our Perception of God's Word:
1. We must consider God's command rather than His chastisement as the motive for application
2. Knowledge carries with it both privilege and responsibility
3. There is no such thing as a nonessential command
4. We must not insist that we will obey only after a seeming contradiction in commandments is resolved

IV. Principles on the Product of Disobedience:
1. Although there is no distinction between sins, there is a difference in consequences
2. Disobedience adds to confusion when adverse circumstances come
3. God's permissive will is entered only through a failure to apply the Scriptures
4. We must refuse to yield to what we know is wrong. Satisfying the drive will only momentarily alleviate the hunger and will stimulate a desire for more
5. Culture cannot serve as an excuse for not obeying God's commands
6. The differences between a trial and a temptation lie in the response

V. Principles on the Life of Application:
1. Circumstances do not indicate God's approval or disapproval

2. The validity of personal application is not dependent on another's acceptance or approval
3. We must resist the temptation to judge others as less spiritual when they do what the Lord has forbidden us to do
4. The path to intellectual excellence is curiosity, investigation, and experimentation; but the path to moral excellence is obedience
5. Our conduct, good or bad, will affect the generations to follow

VI. **Principles on People in the Process of Application:**
1. We must maintain an accountability relationship with a group of people who will exhort us to faith and good works
2. Godly counsel is helpful in the quest of obedience, but it should never be used to avoid personal responsibility

Appendix F
Parallels Between
the Sermon on the Mount and James

James	Sermon on the Mount
Consider it all joy (1: 2-4)	Blessed (5: 3-12)
Wisdom (1: 5-8)	Wise man (7: 24-27)
Uncertainty of riches (1: 9-11)	God's provision (6: 25-34)
Trials (1: 12)	Persecution (5: 10-12)
Temptation (1: 13-15)	Lust (5: 27-30)
Good & Perfect (1: 16-18)	Ask, Seek, Knock (7: 7-12)
Hearing, speaking, anger (1: 19-20)	Anger & murder (5: 21-26)
Doers of the Word (1: 21-25)	Hearing & acting (7: 24-27)
True religion (1: 26-27)	Righteousness (5: 6, 10, 20; 6: 1, 33)
Favoritism (2: 1-7)	Practicing righteousness before men (6: 1)
Royal law (2: 8-13)	Fulfillment of the Law (5: 21-48)
Faith & works (2: 14-26)	Hearing & acting (7: 24-27)
Teaching & speaking (3: 1-12)	Teaching (5: 2; 7: 29)
Two types of wisdom (3: 13-18)	Wise & foolish man (7: 24-27)
Quarrels & conflicts (4: 1-3)	Anger (5: 1-26)
Humility (4: 4-10)	Beatitudes (5: 3-12)

James	Sermon on the Mount
James	**Sermon on the Mount**
Judging (4: 11-12)	Judging (7: 1-5)
Planning (4: 13-17)	Anxiety (6: 25-34)
Misuse of riches (5: 1-6)....................	Materialism (6: 19-24)
Patience & endurance (5: 7-11).........	Persecution (5: 10-12)
Oathes (5: 12)	Oathes (5: 33-37)
Prayer for the sick (5: 13-18)	Prayer (6: 5-13)
Restoration (5: 19-20)........................	Forgiveness (6: 14-15)

Appendix G
Further Study
Other publications by Paul Leavenworth

(also see www.theconvergencegroup.org for additional resources)

Leadership Development Trilogy:

- *Starting Well* by Richard Clinton and Paul Leavenworth. 2012, Convergence Publishing – for younger emerging leaders

- *Living and Leading Well* by Richard Clinton and Paul Leavenworth. 2012, Convergence Publishing – for mid-life leaders

- *Finishing Well* by Richard Clinton and Paul Leavenworth. 2012, Convergence Publishing - for older experienced leaders

Introduction to Christian Growth Series:

- *Introduction to Discipleship* by Paul Leavenworth, 2014, Convergence Publishing – for younger or new Christians

- *Introduction to Leadership* by Paul Leavenworth, 2014, Convergence Publishing – for younger or new Christians

- *Introduction to Life Planning* by Paul Leavenworth, 2014, Convergence Publishing – for younger or new Christians

Leadership Development Series:

- *The Discipleship and Leadership Workbook* by Paul Leavenworth, 2014, Convergence Publishing – introduction to Leadership Development Series

- *The Bible-Centered Leader Workbook* by Paul Leavenworth, 2010, Convergence Publishing – for younger emerging leaders

- *The Spirit-Empowered Leader Workbook* by Paul Leavenworth, 2010, Convergence Publishing – for younger emerging leaders

- *The Discipleship and Mentoring Workbook* by Paul Leavenworth, 2010, Convergence Publishing – for younger emerging leaders

Finishing Well Series:

- *Finishing Well Workbook* by Paul Leavenworth, 2012, Convergence Publishing – for older experienced Christians

- *The Deep Processing Workbook* by Paul Leavenworth, 2011, Convergence Publishing – for older experienced leaders

- *The Extraordinary Power of a Focused Life* by Paul Leavenworth, 2011, Convergence Publishing – for older experienced leaders

Bible-Centered Leader Series:

- *The Way of the Disciple: A Discovery Learning Approach to the Sermon on the Mount* by Paul Leavenworth, 2015, Convergence Publishing – for Christian leaders who want to go deeper in their Bible knowledge and application

- *The Works of the Disciple: A Discovery Learning Approach to the Epistle of James* by Paul Leavenworth, 2014, Convergence Publishing – for Christian leaders who want to go deeper in their Bible knowledge and application

- **More to come!**

Bibliography: Sources

Bible Study Methods

Arthur, Kay. *How to Study Your Bible*, 1994, Harvest House

Hendricks, Howard and William. *Living By the Book*, 1991, Moody Press

Hendrichsen, Walter and Gayle Jackson. *Studying, Interpreting, and Applying the Bible*, 1990, Zondervan Press

Julian, Ron and J. A. Crabtree and David Crabtree. *The Language of God*, 2001, NavPress

Warren, Rick. *Bible Study Methods*, 2006, Zondervan Press

Bible Study Tools

The Contemporary Parallel New Testament, 1997, Oxford University Press

The International Standard Bible Encyclopedia, Geoffrey W. Bromiley (editor), 1979, Eerdmans Publishing

Elwell, Walter. *Topical Analysis of the Bible*, 1991, Baker Books

Vine, W.E. *Expository Dictionary of Old and New Testament Words*, 1996, Nelson Publishers

Biblical Authority

Boice, James Montgomery. *Standing on the Rock*, 1994, Baker Books

Bruce, F. F. *The Canon of Scripture*, 1988, InterVarsity Press

Bible Overview

MacArthur, John. *The MacArthur Bible Handbook*, 2003, Nelson Publishers

Stedman, Ray. *Adventuring Through the Bible*, 1997, Discovery House

Wilkinson, Bruce. *Talk Thru the Bible*, 1983, Nelson Publishers

Old Testament

Bright, John. *A History of Israel*, 1975, Westminster Press

Geisler, Norman. *A Popular Survey of the Old Testament*, 2003, Prince Press

Wood, Leon. *The Prophets of Israel*, 1979, Baker Books

New Testament

Bright, John. *The Kingdom of God*, 1953, Abingdon Press
Gundry, Robert. *A Survey of the New Testament*, 1981, Zondervan Publishing
Ladd, George Eldon. *A Theology of the New Testament*, 1975, Eerdmans Publishers
Stott, John. *The Cross of Christ*, 1986, InterVarsity Press

Theology

Duffield, Guy. *Foundations of Pentecostal Theology*, 1987, LIFE
Grudem, Wayne. *Bible Doctrine*, 1999, Zondervan Publishing
Packer, James. *Knowing God*, 1973, InterVarsity Press

Apologetics

Corduan, Winfried. *Reasonable Faith*, 1993, Broadman & Holman Publishers
Geisler, Norman. *Christian Apologetics*, 2002, Prince Press

Church History

Cairns, Earle. *Christianity Through the Centuries*, 1982, Zondervan Publishing
    An Endless Line of Splendor, 1986, Tyndale House
Latourette, Kenneth Scott. *A History of Christianity*, Vol. I & II, 2005, Prince Press
Shelley, Bruce. *Church History in Plain Language*, 1995, Nelson Publishers

Kingdom of God:

Barclay, William. *The King and the Kingdom*, 1968, Grand Rapids, MI: Baker Book House
Bright, John. *The Kingdom of God*, 1953, Nashville, TN: Abingdon Press
Ellul, Jacques. *The Presence of the Kingdom*, 1967, New York, NY: Seabury Press
Kirk, Andrew. *The Good News of the Kingdom Coming*, 1983, Downers Grove, IL: IVP
Kraybill, Donald. *The Upside-Down Kingdom*, 1978, Scottsdale, PA: Herald Press
Ladd, George. *The Gospel of the Kingdom*, 1959, Grand Rapids, I: Eerdmans
Ladd, George. *The Presence of the Future*, 1974, Grand Rapids, MI: Eerdmans
Mitton, C.L. *Your Kingdom Come*, 1978, Grand Rapids, MI: Eerdmans

Moltmann, Jorgen. *The Church in the Power of the Spirit*, 1977, London, England: SCM Press

Pannenberg, William. Theology and the Kingdom of God, 1977, Philadelphia, PA: Westminister Press

Ridderbos, J. *The Coming of the Kingdom*, 1962, Nutley, NJ: Presbyterian and Reformed Publishing Company

Snyder, Howard. *The Community of the King*, 1977, Downers Grove, IL: IVP

Toon, Peter. *God's Kingdom for Today*, 1980, Westchester, IL: Cornerstone Books

Vos, Geerhardus. *The Kingdom of God and the Church*, 1972, Phillipsburg, NJ: Presbyterian and Reformed Publishing Company

Discipleship:

Bruce, A.B. *The Training of the Twelve*, 1971, Grand Rapids, MI: Kregel

Coleman, Robert. *The Master Plan of Evangelism*, 1971, Old Tappan, NJ: Revell

Hanks, Billie and Shell, William. *Discipleship*, 1981, Grand Rapids, MI: Zondervan

Ortiz, Juan Carlos. *Call to Discipleship*, 1975, Plainfield, NJ: Logos

    Disciple, 1975, Carol Stream, IL: Creation House

Phillips, Keith. *The Making of a Disciple*, 1981 , Old Tappan, NJ: Revell

Schaeffer, Francis. *The Mark of the Christian*, 1970, Downers Grove, IL: IVP

Sider, Ronald. *Rich Christians in an Age of Hunger*, 1984, Downers Grove, IL: IVP

Sine, Tom. *The Mustard Seed Conspiracy*, 1981 , Waco, TX: Word

Watson, David. *Called and Committed*, 1982, Wheaton, IL: Shaw

Yoder, John Howard. *The Politics of Jesus*, 1972, Grand Rapids, MI: Eerdmans

Simplicity:

Foster, Richard J. *Freedom of Simplicity*, 1981, New York, NY: Harper & Row

Gish, Arthur G. *Beyond the Rat Race*, 1973, Scottsdale, PA: Herald Press

Sider, Ronald J. *Lifestyles in the Eighties*, 1982, Philadelphia, PA: Westminster

    Rich Christians in an Age of Hunger, 1984, Downers Grove, IL: IVP

Sine, Tom. *The Mustard Seed Conspiracy*, 1981, Waco, TX: Word

Christian Views of War and Peace:

Bernbaum, John (ed.) *Perspectives on Peacemaking*, 1984, Ventura, CA: Regal

Clouse, Robert (ed.) *War: Four Christian Views*, 1981, Downers Grove, IL: IVP

Craigie, Peter C. *The Problem of War in the Old Testament*, 1978, Grand Rapids, MI: Eerdmans

Culver, Robert D. *The Peace-Mongers*, 1985, Wheaton, IL: Tyndale

Lapp, John A. (ed.) *Peacemakers in a Broken World*, 1969, Scottsdale, PA: Herald

Holmes, Arthur (ed.) *War and Christian Ethics*, 1975, Grand Rapids, MI: Baker

Yoder, John H. *The Original Revolution*, 1977, Scottsdale, PA: Herald

Leadership:

Barna, George (editor). *Leaders on Leadership*, 1997, Regal Books

Blackaby, Henry and Richard Blackaby. *Spiritual Leadership*, 2001, Broadman and Holman Publishers

Clinton, J. Robert. *The Making of a Leader*, 1988, NavPress

Malphurs, Aubrey. *Being Leaders*, 2003, Baker Books

Maxwell, John. *Leadership Gold*, 2008, Nelson Publishers

Sanders, J. Oswald. *Spiritual Leadership*, 1994, Moody Press

ABOUT THE AUTHOR

Dr. Paul G. Leavenworth

Educational Background

Graduate: Ed. D. Counseling (1984), College of William and Mary, Williamsburg, VA
M. Ed. Guidance and Counseling (1979), Whitworth College, Spokane, WA
M.A. Theology (1976), Fuller Theological Seminary, Pasadena, CA

Undergraduate: B.S. Liberal Studies (1972), Oregon State University, Corvallis, OR

Professional Experience

Higher Education/Teaching:
Instructor/Student Development Counselor (1992-1998); Adjunct Instructor
(1998-present), Eugene Bible College/New Hope College, Eugene, OR
Higher Education/Administration:
Acting Dean (1986-87)/Associate Dean of Student Development (1984-87), Houghton
College, Houghton, NY
Associate Dean of Students (1981-83)/Assistant Dean of Students (1980-81), Franklin
and Marshall College, Lancaster, PA

Church and Missions:

Executive Director for Leadership Development and Church Ministries (1998-2009),
Open Bible Churches, Des Moines, IA
Missionary (1990-92), Youth With a Mission (YWAM) – NorCal, Richardson Springs, CA
Associate Pastor/Educational Ministries (1988-90), Vineyard Christian Fellowship,
Anaheim, CA
Assistant Pastor (1973-74), Scott Valley Berean Church, Etna, CA

Coaching and Consulting:

Executive Director (2010-present), the Convergence group, West Des Moines, IA

Dissertation

"Differences in Psychological Types of Student Leaders and Non-Leaders at a Private Liberal Arts
College," May 1984, in partial fulfillment of requirements for the degree of Doctor of Education in
Counseling from the College of William and Mary in Virginia.

Made in the USA
Middletown, DE
05 June 2021